The Skimobile Express gives today's skiers and riders a swift and scenic ride to the top of Cranmore Mountain, adding up to more runs and fine views. *Photo by Bill Lee, Cranmore Mountain Resort.*

THE HISTORY OF CRANMORE MOUNTAIN

TOM EASTMAN

THE History PRESS

Published by The History Press
Charleston, SC 29403
www.historypress.net

First published 2012
Second printing 2013

Manufactured in the United States

ISBN 978.1.60949.910.5

Library of Congress CIP data applied for.

Notice: The information in this book is true and complete to the best of our knowledge. It is offered without guarantee on the part of the author or The History Press. The author and The History Press disclaim all liability in connection with the use of this book.

CONTENTS

FOREWORD

FLIGHT WITHOUT WINGS

It was a sunny, February afternoon in 1989, and Cranmore ski conditions were perfect during the resort's "Flight Without Wings" weeklong event, celebrating the fiftieth anniversary of the arrival of Austrian ski great Hannes Schneider from Nazi captivity in Europe.

I reached for the phone and quickly dialed Tom Eastman, author of the then–recently published *Flight Without Wings: A Celebration of Hannes Schneider and 50 Years of Skiing at Mt. Cranmore*, to explain that Herbert Schneider had convinced Toni Matt—famed Austrian ski champion who schussed the Tuckerman Headwall to win the 1939 Inferno Race a full minute faster than the second-place finisher, and who hadn't skied in years—to take a few ski runs that afternoon. Did Tom want to join us?

Ever the faithful and consummate scribe for Mount Washington Valley news and events, and in the midst of finishing an article about our fiftieth anniversary event, Tom declined. "Rice, you rat!" he said. "I'm on deadline, but I want a raincheck!"

Toni demanded we satisfy a condition before he would board the chairlift. Cranmore's new ski rental fleet was supplied by Rossignol, and Toni would *not* ski on a French ski! A quick search among ski instructors and patrollers turned up a pair of Austrian-made Kastle skis, and soon I was sharing a chairlift ride with Herbert and Toni, two ski giants from the early days of modern skiing pioneered by Herbert's bigger-than-life father, Hannes.

While Toni used a cane and walked with a limp, once on skis it was as if he shed thirty years and returned to top athletic form. Herbert and Toni—best friends since childhood, and both then in their late sixties—were soon carving big GS turns at high speed. I hustled to keep pace behind them, honored to ski with this famous pair but fearful I would catch an edge and not only suffer the embarrassment of a fall but also see them ski off without me. I remember watching in awe as these men linked aggressive side-by-side turns in perfect harmony.

Three months later, we heard the sad news that Toni had passed away. Just a week before, I had sent Toni a photo of himself, Herbert and me standing together after our ski run in February. I'd asked him if he would please autograph it for me next to Herbert's signature. Later that summer, a package arrived containing the photo with Toni's signature next to Herbert's. His family noted it was one of the last tasks he performed at his desk.

This recollection is but one of many from Cranmore's 50th anniversary of the Schneiders' arrival that I hold dear. Now, this historic ski resort is celebrating its 75th. Much has occurred since the 50th to further burnish Cranmore's prominent ski industry reputation, including new ski and snowboarding terrain; major expansion of Cranmore's snow-making system; installation of a high-speed detachable summit lift; growth of its already legendary ski and snowboard teaching programs; and bold expansion into summer operations with a mountain coaster, zip lines, summer tubing and much more. I have no doubt that Cranmore's growth and success will continue as it looks ahead from its 75th year toward its 100th!

Stephen K. Rice
October 13, 2012

Stephen K. Rice is senior vice-president and managing director for CNL Financial Group, the Florida-based company that provided the capital for the purchase of Cranmore in June 2010 by Brian and Tyler Fairbank and Joe O'Donnell. From 1987 to 1989, he served as marketing director at the resort.

ACKNOWLEDGEMENTS

On a personal level, I dedicate this book to Herbert Schneider, who patiently never tired of this writer's questions over the years, whether on the slopes at Cranmore or in the village streets of his and Hannes's hometown of St. Anton am Arlberg.

To get to go to Austria would be a treat for any ski history enthusiast. To get to go with Herbert, as I did with Jeff Leich of the New England Ski Museum and others in 2005 for a ski history conference on the fiftieth anniversary of Hannes Schneider's death, was priceless.

I thank Leich and historian E. John B. Allen of the New England Ski Museum for their assistance with this book, as well as all others who have donated their time and photographs, especially Stefi Reed Hastings and Doris and Herbert Schneiders' sons, Hannes and Christoph. I also thank Lydia Lansing for her editorial guidance and Bob Cottrell of the Conway Public Library and Andrea Masters of the North Conway Library. I also am indebted to Mark Butterfield of the Gibson-Woodbury Foundation; author Jeremy Davis of the New England Lost Ski Areas Project; Barbara Smith, widow of late photographer Dick Smith; and modern photographers Drew Phillips, Bill Lee, Jamie Gemmiti, Lloyd Jones and Brooks Dodge III. Thanks go to Austrian historians Christof Thony and Thomas Ebster of the Arlberg region. Former Cranmore marketing director Steve Rice, now of CNL

Financial Group, has been an invaluable help and Cranmore supporter over the years. I would like to thank Cranmore president and general manager Ben Wilcox, marketing director Kathy Bennett and staff, as well as the new Fairbank-O'Donnell ownership team for asking me to do this book—it was an honor.

I thank my dear sister, Jeanie Eastman Ryan, who has helped with the production and copy editing, always being a good sounding board. We come from a large, Irish storytelling family where a love of sports, especially New England skiing, is a gift we continue to enjoy together today. I salute in particular my late brother, Steve Eastman (1949–2008), with whom I worked at the *Mountain Ear* from 1979 to 2007, covering the local ski scene, as well as my oldest brother, Dave Eastman, for putting me in touch with such early ski history mentors as the late Dick May. I would like to thank Publisher Mark Guerringue and all my colleagues at the *Conway Daily Sun*, where I have hung my skis and filed my stories since 2007, just down the road from Cranmore's beckoning slopes.

I hope you'll agree that despite the changes of time and the passing of many of the original characters and interviewees, the Cranmore story then and now is an exciting one. North Conway is a historic ski town with a ski heritage, as noted in the 2011–12 *National Geographic* "Top 25 List" of best ski towns in the world.

Cranmore is an original. Cranmore early on set the bar for skiing, the soul-freeing sport and lifestyle, which Hannes Schneider once referred to as "Flight Without Wings."

May you enjoy the read, and remember when you take your next run to do as Hannes always directed his skiing students: "Bend ze knees."

INTRODUCTION TO CRANMORE

A RICH SKI HERITAGE

Any good story always has a hero who is aided by his helpers as they battle the arch villain so that the forces of good can prevail over evil. I've always felt that the story of Cranmore is a great one to tell because it has at its core all of those ingredients.

First is the compelling tale of Austrian ski great Hannes Schneider (1890–1955), the renowned "Father of Modern Skiing" and the undisputed leader at the time of the skiing world, who was arrested in the Austrian Anschluss of March 1938 for his anti-Nazi views and held under house arrest in Germany. Enter into the plot the supporting roles of the local good guys, Eastern Slope Ski School/ski shop founder Carroll P. Reed (1905–1995), and Cranmore developer, North Conway native, New York banker and world financier Harvey Dow Gibson (1882–1950). Add such other heroes as Hannes's son, fellow U.S. Ski Hall of Famer and longtime former owner/general manager Herbert Schneider (1920–2012); his best friend, Austrian ski racer and early instructor Toni Matt (1920–1989), winner of the legendary 1939 Mount Washington Inferno; and the quirky mechanical genius of Skimobile inventor George Morton (d. 1961) and his son, Parker (d. 1991). The good guys, with the Schneiders, Gibson and Reed in the starring roles, versus the bad guys, led by Adolf Hitler (1889–1945), the notorious arch villain of the twentieth century.

Cranmore skimeister Hannes Schneider (1890–1955) executes a ge·län·de·sprung in the Alps. *Schneider Family Files.*

Home to the famous Gibson Cup from 1940 to 1966, Cranmore also has a celebrated racing heritage. Among the top local racers who have honed their skills at Cranmore over the years are such Olympians as Paula Kann Valar (1948); Imogene Opton Fish (1952); Brooks Dodge (1952 and '56); David Currier, Terry Palmer and Tyler Palmer (all 1972); Abbi Fisher (1976 and 1980); and current U.S. Team member Leanne Smith (2010). Many other former Eastern Slope Ski Club Junior Program local skiers have gone on to the collegiate and national levels.

Since 1938, all Junior Program skiers have been given an opportunity to learn a lifelong sport—something that both Hannes and Herbert Schneider held dear to their hearts.

The sunny, hometown ski area has been sold six times over the past seventy-five years. Cranmore is seeing a rebirth under the new ownership, with $8.3 million invested in both winter and year-round amenities. They are the new heroes in the Cranmore story.

This is a story that never grows old—the birth and cultivation of modern skiing in the United States at Cranmore.

CHAPTER 1

CRANMORE'S BEGINNINGS

SEVENTY-FIVE YEARS OF SKIING—PLUS TWO YEARS

Seventy-five years ago, developer Harvey D. Gibson rented a rope tow from Carroll Reed in Jackson and moved it to Cranmore for the 1937–38 season, one year before the start of the Skimobile. This marked the in-town mountain's start as a lift-serviced area, but its beginnings as a ski place predate that to the winter of 1935–36, when the 1935-founded Eastern Slope Ski Club cleared a trail, according to "History of the Eastern Slope Ski Club, 1936–2006."

Many have asked over the years just how Cranmore got its name and whether it was ever known as Lookout Mountain and later renamed Cranmore when Gibson bought the west face of the mountain in January 1937. Although some may give credit to Gibson for renaming Cranmore, historical research shows that it was known as Cranmore long before he acquired it. It may be the case that Lookout Point was the name for a part of the mountain that came to be known as Cranmore, according to volunteer researcher Lorena Hoyt of the Conway Public Library's Henney History Room.

In the fall of 2012, Hoyt said that nineteenth-century maps show the mountain as having an area known as Lookout Point. As for being called "Cranmore," she said that a farmer named John E. Cranmore moved from Bartlett to North Conway in 1857. He had a son (also named John E.

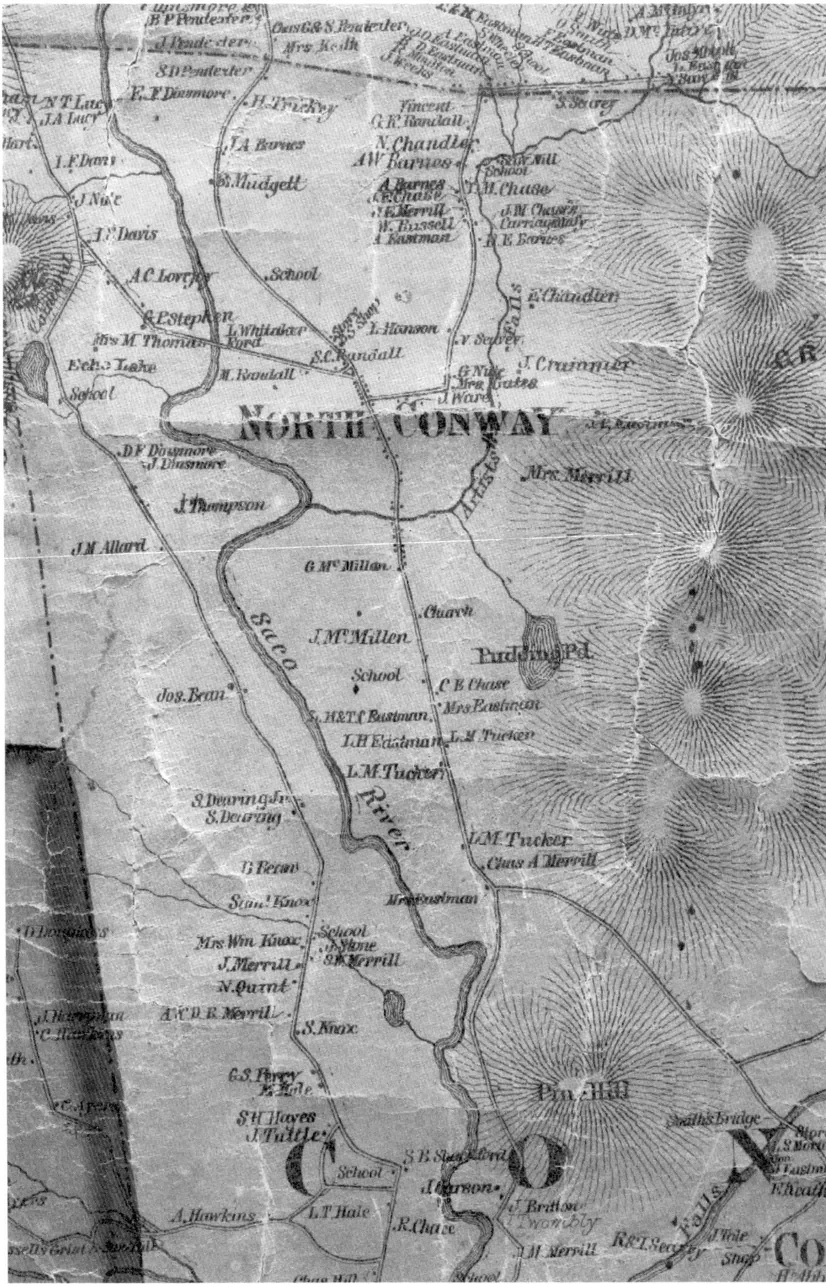

How did Cranmore Mountain get its name? Historians say that the name may have come from two nineteenth-century Conway farmers, a father and son, both named John E. Cranmore. This 1860 map shows the name on the mountain as Crammer (right), although spelling mistakes were commonly made on nineteenth-century maps, according to Lorena Hoyt of the Conway Public Library's Henney History Room. *Courtesy of Conway Public Library.*

Cranmore) who built a house in Kearsarge that was still standing as of 2012 next to the Ski-Bees Ski Club.

In addition, said Hoyt, one or both of the Cranmores also owned farmland that extended from Artist Falls Road in North Conway to the base of the Green Hills between E. Chandler, Esq., and an Eastman. The 1860 inventory said he had a homestead farm with buildings thereon valued at $400, with two cows valued at $40 and one horse valued at $20.

An 1860 map lists the property as "Crammer," but Hoyt says spelling mistakes were commonly made on old maps. She asserted that the town inventory for that year clearly and consistently had the name as Cranmore, as does the 1860 Federal Census and the 1892 Hurd map for New Hampshire. Locals called the area to which they hiked Lookout Point, as it is depicted on a U.S. Geological Survey (USGS) University of New Hampshire map from 1896, Hoyt said, with no mention of Crammer or Cranmore. It next appears on a USGS map in 1942 as Cranmore, according to the Henney Room's historical map collection.

Gibson (1882–1950) grew up in a house not far from Cranmore on Artist Falls Road (at the time of this writing, it is still standing, located at the juncture of Artist Falls Road and the 2002-built North-South Road and owned by G.B. Carrier Corp.). In his 1951 autobiography, published a year after his death, Gibson wrote that he "remembered clearly the days as a boy I used to coast at Mt. Cranmore, located just on the border of North Conway Village."

Common Lands?

Aside from the name issue, there has long been local discussion about how Gibson acquired Cranmore. In response to a reporter's queries, attorney Peter G. Hastings of Hastings Law Firm of Fryeburg in fall 2012 said he conducted extensive title search work for Cranmore's then owners in the 1960s. That research showed that Gibson acquired most of the west side of the mountain in 1937 by buying shares for nine parcels from some of the descendants of Conway's sixty-nine original settlers who had used the Green Hills for common lands for maple sugaring, firewood harvesting and sheep grazing.

Given the number of heirs involved through the years from the original sixty-nine settlers and their shares of the Common Lands, there was some confusion as to who owned what, Hastings said. "The way I always heard the story," said Hastings, "is that after they built the Upper Skimobile [in August 1939], there was some question about just who owned the land at the top."

According to Hastings, Gibson held deeds to the Chandler lot and Chandler Sugar Orchard, plus the Thomas Merrill Grant, collectively forming one tract on the upper western face and top of Cranmore Mountain. He said common lands farther north and adjacent to the parcel set over to Cranmore remained undefined as to ownership for many years but now are a Conway Town Forest.

Abutter Redstone Properties Inc.—which ran the Redstone quarry and had bought sixty-one common shares—and Gibson's widow went to Carroll County Superior Court to file what Hastings termed a "friendly lawsuit" to try to settle the matter for both parties' interests.

"[Mrs.] Gibson (Cranmore Skimobiles Inc.) and Redstone Properties went to Carroll County Superior Court in Ossipee…with this action called a 'friendly bill in equity to quiet title,' to partition the land," said Hastings. "They were not contesting each other's holdings. It was done to clear it up. They published a notice in the newspapers, and no one objected," said Hastings, noting that Waldo Seavey of Lovell, Maine, surveyed the property as part of the court proceedings. "The court set aside 400 to 500 acres to Cranmore," Hastings said, "and maybe 800 to 1,000 to Redstone Properties. Each agreed that they would have the reciprocal right to the other's land: Cranmore had the right to ski and make trails over Redstone's land, and Redstone had the rights to mine on Cranmore's property. That is how they got title to it."

The court made its ruling in September 1951, the year after Harvey Gibson's death. Gibson's claims to the west side and summit were affirmed, Hastings said. In addition, the court agreed to the parties' plans regarding other shares and uses.

"The decision by Carroll County Superior Court is recorded in the registry at Book 280, Page 267 through 276," said Hastings. "However, there were further agreements made between the two parties allowing skiing and trams over Redstone Properties' land as drained by Artist Falls Brook and reciprocally Redstone Properties reserved mineral rights over Cranmore land," wrote Hastings in an October 11, 2012 e-mail.

The Beginning

As to Cranmore's early years for skiing, the *Reporter* newspaper of January 28, 1937, contained two articles regarding the mountain, both on page three. The first proclaimed, "Boys Build Ski Shelter on Cranmore Mountain," and another announced, "Harvey D. Gibson Buys Cranmore Mountain for Public Use."

The first article was accompanied by a photograph, showing a cabin that was completed in early winter 1936–37 at the base of today's South Slope by six local boys. The boys included future ski instructor and eventual physician William G. Duprey Jr., Ken Lucy, Robert Bly, Neil Cates Jr., Kenneth Kenison and David Stiles. Early ski supporter Edna Ricker, co-operator of Kearsarge Hall of North Conway with her sister, Mary Kinney, supplied the building materials for the small log cabin. Located just above a rock, which now bears a plaque dedicated to the memory of Harvey and Helen Gibson, the cabin had a wood stove and also sold hot dogs and hot coffee to hungry skiers during that winter of 1936–37.

"These boys," read the copy, alluding to work made by the 1935-founded Eastern Slope Ski Club, "are members of the larger group which first cleared the trail last year and, this year widened and extended it. The use of the land, up to this week was made public through the generosity of Miss Nellie McGrail, the former owner. With a foot of snow it is considered an excellent novice trail."

Right below that short story on the cabin is the story about Gibson's acquisition of the mountain. "Announcement," the story said, "has been made of the purchase, this week, of all the private land on Cranmore Mountain by Harvey D. Gibson, the former owner being Miss Nellie McGrail. While the land will not be given outright to the town, it was purchased and will be further developed for public use. The mountain at present is the site of a trail and shelter, mentioned above. Men will be put to work shortly on further developments, the details of which will be revealed at a later date. This," the brief, two-paragraph article adds, "is only one of many instances of Mr. Gibson's interests in his hometown, and his desire to assist in its progress."

Other stories on the same page of the *Reporter* included "Eastern Slope Langlauf and Slalom Competitions Will Definitely Be Held" regarding a January 30 race planned for Russell's Golf Course in Kearsarge and "Eastern Slope Draws Dartmouth Skiers."

As the *Reporter* stories illustrated, things were happening on the ski front in the Eastern Slope Region—and Cranmore as we know it was about to take shape.

The first White Mountain Winter Carnival (with ski jumping) was held in North Conway in 1922. The Boston and Maine Railroad began its snow trains to North Conway in 1932; American Inferno Races had been held in Tuckerman Ravine in 1933 and 1934; the Civilian Conservation Corps had cut many local trails such as the Wildcat beginning in 1933; Moody's Farm in Jackson had opened its overhead cable tow in 1935; the Eastern Slope Ski Club (ESSC) had been established in December 1935; Bill and Betty Whitney had bought Moody's in fall 1936; Carroll Reed's Ski School had been founded in Jackson in December 1936; and now, in January 1937, Gibson was buying Cranmore.

This is all good to contemplate as Cranmore celebrates its seventy-fifth anniversary and we take a look back at some of the individuals who played central roles over the years in the development of skiing there as well as in the region.

CHAPTER 2

RIDING THE SNOW TRAINS OF OLD

Skiers and snowboarders of today have no idea of the romance and fun they missed out on by not having been around when snow trains used to ride the rails, bringing skiers and snowsports enthusiasts to the pioneering winter playgrounds of New England from the 1930s to the early 1950s.

Credit for the idea of a snow train should be shared among Appalachian Mountain Club (AMC) members, former Dartmouth Outing Club president Carl Shumway and Frederick T. Grant, passenger agent of the Boston & Maine (B&M) Railroad. In the 1920s, the ski gained some acceptance as an alternative to the snowshoe for winter forays on AMC club trips. The AMC's first ski trip was in February 1925, and weekly ski trips were scheduled in the winter of 1927. Shumway may have tried to get the B&M interested in the idea in 1929 or 1930.

AMC member John Holden, who saw ski train excursions in Munich, reported on the concept at a club meeting, and Park Carpenter, another of the early club skiers, brought the idea to the Boston & Maine Railroad, which was desperate to rebuild its faltering ridership. The first trip was run in January 1931 to Warner, New Hampshire, and more than eight thousand riders were counted that first season.

In that first season, the B&M relied on Shumway for advice on where to send its weekly excursions, according to a 1936 article in the *Boston Evening*

The first Boston & Maine snow train went from Boston to Warner, New Hampshire, in 1931. Snow trains began taking skiers to North Conway in 1932. When gas rationing made it infeasible to drive to other areas during World War II, Cranmore's accessibility helped its business boom during that period, since skiers could ride trains to North Conway and then walk to the mountain's slopes. *Courtesy of Dwight Smith.*

Transcript. Shumway's grandson, Bo Adams, is currently president of New England Ski Museum.

Soon, the snow trains became a fixture of the winter landscape of New England, running from early December to mid-March every season, with trains departing from New York City, New Haven, Boston and Portland and arriving at such destinations as the Berkshires in western Massachusetts and Laconia, Plymouth, Whitefield, Ossipee, North Conway and Intervale, New Hampshire.

The first snow train on the Conway Branch from Boston ran in 1932, according to Dwight Smith, former Conway Scenic Railroad president. When Mount Cranmore opened for its first season in 1937–38, snow trains helped bring skiers from Boston to fill its slopes. The war years of the early 1940s found as many as five trains coming into North Conway on a Sunday, carrying up to four thousand skiers for a one-day trip.

The weekend snow trains operated on Friday nights, bringing an additional seven to eight hundred passengers to North Conway and leaving on Sunday with their passengers well satiated after a weekend of skiing, skating, tobogganing, singing and dancing.

"At times," Smith noted once, "there were too many trains on hand for North Conway's rail yard, and the overflow trains would be 'deadheaded'—sent empty—to the Maine Central's yard in nearby Bartlett for servicing and towing."

Snow trains were promoted through posters designed by artists of the era. Romance, adventure and fun were all part of the experience. *Courtesy of New England Ski Museum.*

Each of the Boston & Maine trains was manned by members of the Passenger Traffic Department, who wore dark blue suits that featured the B&M's small red insignia on their shirtsleeves. The guides offered advice on where to ski and what to wear, giving skiers an insider's account of the conditions at the slopes of New England.

The destinations each week were no hit-or-miss propositions, according to the B&M public relations department. Each week, a network of north country observers would telegraph snow reports, which were printed in *Ski Bulletin*, one of the first serial ski publications in the country. The *Ski Bulletin* was started by AMC members and was not only useful for choosing snow train destinations but was also circulated to a growing list of subscribers who planned weekend trips based on its reports. Based on that data, a decision on where to head would be made on a Thursday. That decision would then be posted in all the Boston newspapers the

Skiers wax up their skis inside the Boston & Maine ski train en route to the mountains in 1946. *Courtesy of Dwight Smith.*

next day (as well as in Worcester papers when trains were leaving from or passing through there).

For those who didn't own their own equipment, the B&M took care of skiers through its fully stocked "Winter Sports Car." Maintained by the Armstrong Company of Boston, the car was parked on Track 3 at Boston's North Station on weekdays. It would be coupled with the snow trains for the trips north.

Like the $4.35 ticket fare for a round trip, the rental rates were more than reasonable at the snow car—a skier in 1936 could rent a pair of skis with leather bindings for $1.00, or $1.25 with metal bindings. Boots rented for $1.00 a pair, and all lengths of ski poles went for $0.50 a pair. Snowshoes were also available, as were all manner of winter clothing (mittens, ski parkas and more). Railroad officials boasted that the cars were well warmed, making them ideal "homes for the day."

Given the youthfulness of most of their passengers, the snow trains acquired a reputation over the years for their spiritedness. But some longtime

In this publicity shot from the Boston & Maine in 1946, sleepy skiers head home after a long day on the slopes at Mount Cranmore in North Conway. Each of the Boston & Maine trains was manned by members of the Passenger Traffic Department, who wore dark blue ski suits that featured the B&M's smart red insignia on their coat sleeves. The guides offered advice on where to ski and what to wear, giving skiers an insider's account of the New England ski slopes, according to a 1937 snow train brochure. *Courtesy of Dwight Smith.*

railroad officials said that reputation was somewhat overstated. "Sure, there were some rowdies who came up for the ride," the late Henry Gagnon, a retired B&M conductor, said in an interview in 1989, "but not many. Overall, they were skiers, and nice kids."

Added the late Fran Johnson, a longtime former Cranmore office worker, "It wasn't like that all the time. But certainly, if you saw beer bottles in the windows of the cars when you got to North Station for the trip north, you knew the trip was going to be a bit rowdy." She said it wasn't the skiers who were the cause of the trouble—it was the day-trippers along for a good time.

Unlike other areas such as Whitneys' Hill in Jackson, which had no railroad service, Cranmore's proximity to the North Conway Train Station served it well during those war years, as GIs on furlough could ride the rails in the gas-rationing days and then easily walk to Cranmore or be transported by wagon. As a result, Cranmore boomed during the war years.

After the war, new and larger resorts opened out West. Americans enjoyed the postwar boom years, and the automobile and improved highways changed the way the public traveled. Trains took the hit.

The B&M ran its last regular snow train in 1950, although there were sporadic attempts to revive the excursions, including one in 1956 that carried only seventy-three passengers. The B&M stopped all passenger service between Boston and North Conway in December 1961 and ran its last freight run in October 1972. The railroad filed a request to abandon the West Ossipee to North Conway and Intervale line in 1971, a request that was granted by the Interstate Commerce Commission in 1973.

In the late 1960s and early '70s, an annual excursion run for those who had ridden the snow trains in the old days was held by the Massachusetts Bay Railroad Enthusiasts Inc., a rail-fan club based in Boston. Among those who rode a Buddliner on one of those excursions to North Conway in February 1968 was Dwight Smith, a rail fan and twenty-one-year veteran of the B&M freight traffic department. The 1874-built, Russian-style North Conway station had been boarded up and was in danger of being sold to an outside developer but had been bought by local Yield House founder Bill Levy and ski shop founder Carroll Reed. It was Reed who had founded the region's first ski school as the American branch of Hannes Schneider's St. Anton, Austria school in Jackson in December 1936 and who subsequently sold his Jackson and Cranmore ski schools to Gibson. Gibson, in turn, put Schneider in charge of the schools as part of his plan to bring Schneider to Cranmore after winning his release from the Nazis in February 1939.

When Smith saw the station on that rail-fans trip in 1968, he envisioned transforming it as the centerpiece of a plan to operate a tourist line in the Conways. Reed and Levy approved the idea, and the Conway Scenic Railroad came into being in 1974.

Perhaps the most famous of all snow train passengers was Hannes Schneider, who rode the rails with his family to North Conway, arriving on the morning of February 11, 1939. After Hannes's release from Nazi captivity, which Cranmore developer and world financier Harvey Dow Gibson had managed to arrange, Gibson and his wife met the Schneiders in New York Harbor following their passage across the Atlantic on the *Queen Mary*. After a ride on the night train from New York, in front of the North Conway station, residents welcomed the Schneiders to their new home.

So, skiing and railroading go together in North Conway's case very well, indeed, as their histories are intertwined. All ABBOAAARD!

CHAPTER 3
CARROLL P. REED
SKI SCHOOL VISIONARY

Inducted posthumously into the U.S. Ski Hall of Fame in 2002, Carroll P. Reed (1905–1995) was an exceptionally community-minded man whose vision helped to launch organized ski instruction in the Eastern Slope Region in New Hampshire's eastern White Mountains with the introduction of his ski school in Jackson, New Hampshire, in December 1936.

Although felled by an accident in which he broke his back while skiing the Wildcat Trail in April 1934, he subsequently had the magnanimity and forethought to found his ski school, reasoning that if America had ski schools similar to those in Europe, there would be less chance of others injuring themselves and ending up like him.

Reed will probably always be better known as the namesake of the Carroll Reed's clothing and sporting goods store he founded in Jackson in the fall of 1937 than as an early ski promoter. He and his wife, Kay (Damon) Reed (1916–1999), worked tirelessly as partners in building Carroll Reed's, which they sold in 1969, but skiing and the ski school remained Carroll's passionate concern, even after he sold the school in fall 1938.

As longtime skier Dick May (1915–1999) of Jackson said in an interview in August 1983, the lack of recognition previously due Reed for his skiing contributions is partly attributable to Carroll's own modesty. May—who worked for Reed in the winter of 1938–39 by helping to manage his

Carroll P. Reed

Carroll P. Reed (1905–1995) was a Boston insurance worker who skied often in the early 1930s. After breaking his back on a ski run in April 1934 on the Wildcat Trail built by the Civilian Conservation Corps in 1933, Reed had to undergo surgery. While recuperating, he read an article about ski schools in Europe. That gave him the idea of launching a ski school. He founded the Eastern Slope Ski School, American Branch of the Hannes Schneider Ski School in Jackson, New Hampshire in December 1936 and founded his ski shop the following year. *Courtesy of Stefi Reed Hastings.*

shop in what is now the North Conway 5 and 10 Store—cited Reed's business acumen in establishing the region's first ski school, as well as his ability to harness the support of influential individuals in the community for the endeavor.

"There were a lot of key pioneers who helped get skiing going around here [in the Eastern Slope Region], but I've always given credit to Carroll for attracting the interest of such heavy hitters as Harvey Gibson, Noel Wellman, Dr. Harold Shedd and Chuck Emerson to really make it take hold," said May, a former public relations director at Thorn and Wildcat ski areas and a veteran of the Tenth Mountain Division Ski Troops of World War II fame. "Carroll had the initial concept, although he probably [wouldn't] tell you that out of modesty," May added.

SKIING WITH ABANDON

Reed's family came from the Bath area on the Maine coast. Raised in Boston, Massachusetts, and never wealthy while growing up, Reed helped his family in high school during the Great Depression years by going to the country, gathering eggs from farmers, washing them and then helping his father sell them. He was working for John Hancock Insurance in that city and attending night school at Boston University when he took his first ski trip to the White Mountains in the early 1930s.

Staying at Moody's Farm in Jackson—later known as Whitneys' Inn after skiers Bill and Betty Whitney bought it in the fall of 1936—Reed and his colleagues took to the early ski trails and farm pastures that dotted the Wildcat River Valley with the hellbent abandon and energy of youth, honing their technique from their mistakes.

In 1933, he and fellow Boston-based ski enthusiasts formed a ski club, the White Mountain Ski Runners. (In 1993, the club—which now has a ski house in North Conway—honored Reed with a proclamation on the club's sixtieth anniversary, noting that "as a founder, you promoted the sport of skiing and the members of this club benefited greatly from your efforts and generosity.")

Reed and his fellow ski enthusiasts in those days already had a number of trails on which to practice their sport. One of the Great Depression's consequences was the development of the Civilian Conservation Corps (CCC). Several divisions of the CCC were sent to the White Mountains, and along with other projects, they cut ski trails throughout the region.

The original sign of the Eastern Slope Ski School, which hung outside the school's first office at what today is the Wildcat Inn in Jackson, was created by local craftsman Rodney Woodward. He also designed the ESSS logo in the center. Late ski instructor J. Arthur Doucette of Jackson salvaged the sign years later from a lumberyard scrap pile. It is now at the New England Ski Museum. *Courtesy of New England Ski Museum.*

Among the areas that Reed and like-minded ski pioneers could schuss were the famous Wildcat Trail on Wildcat Mountain, the Tuckerman Ravine Fire Trail on Mount Washington and trails on Mount Chocorua, Bear Mountain in Bartlett, Mount Bartlett in Intervale and Black Mountain and Doublehead in Jackson.

"We'd load up a car and come up here for weekends and take over four or five rooms at Moody's Farm—they served unbelievable breakfasts and dinners," Reed related, adding, "My group skied mostly up in Pinkham Notch. We just skied in those days. We didn't have any conception of style."

After climbing and skiing Mount Chocorua on April 21, 1934, Reed and his companions headed north to Pinkham Notch to finish their day of schussing on the notorious Wildcat Ski Trail. On the last run, as the sun was setting behind Mount Washington, the soft corn snow turned to ice, and at a spot where a brook ran from the woods across the trail, the conditions were particularly icy. Reed, then twenty-nine, was the group's leadoff man.

"It was wonderful corn snow in the morning, but by that last run, it had turned to patchy ice, and I was tired," Reed recalled. He hit the patch of ice full tilt. Losing control, his skis came out from under him, and he careened off the trail into a tree. The accident broke Reed's back and paralyzed him from the waist down immediately. In those pre-ski-lift days, there was no such thing as a ski patrolman—just concerned fellow skiers.

Eventually, they were able to drag a toboggan up from the bottom of the mountain and carry the injured Reed down the icy, rough trail to a truck, which transported him to Memorial Hospital in North Conway. A week after being operated on by a neurosurgeon brought up from Massachusetts General, the feeling in Reed's legs began to return. It wasn't until nineteen weeks later, however, that he was able to leave the facility—on crutches.

Envisions Ski School

While laid up, Reed read in an issue of *Appalachia Journal* about European ski schools. Written by early American racer Tom Cabot, it focused on the largest and most famous school in the world, the Hannes Schneider Ski School in St. Anton, Austria. The story predicted that ski schools would, in time, also proliferate in the United States.

Intrigued, Reed began thinking about a ski school in the Conway area. Told by former Olympic skier/Dartmouth graduate Charlie Proctor that Jackson was an ideal spot to locate a school because of the blow-over of snow from Mount Washington, Reed decided that the time for a ski school in the area had arrived. As soon as he was able, he set about the task of convincing others to share in his endeavor.

"I felt that the ski school could accomplish two major goals," Reed recalled. If others could learn to ski properly, he noted, then perhaps the risk of skiing accidents similar to his would be lessened. Furthermore, the sport needed the influx of knowledgeable instructors from Europe in order to continue developing. This growth, in turn, would benefit the slow winter economy of the local mountain villages.

It was a good idea, but Reed had to spend yet another year and a half recovering from his accident. By the summer of 1936, he had formulated his plan for the establishment of the Eastern Slope Ski School, a name he was allowed to use by the then-one-year-old Eastern Slope Ski Club. He enlisted the support of the club's leaders, most notably Dr. Harold Shedd, Chuck Emerson, Phil Robertson, Bob Davis, Noel Wellman and Jimmy and Gladys Carter. One of the earliest ski clubs in the country, the ESSC was devoted to promoting skiing in the region, and its members enthusiastically threw their support behind Reed's ski school proposal.

Ski Shop Business

Concurrent with his plans for a ski school, Reed—who after the accident made the mountains his home—also became involved with the retail aspects of the ski business in the fall of 1936. Saks Fifth Avenue opened ski stores in Sun Valley, Idaho, and Jackson that year, and Reed was hired to run the latter shop at a salary of twenty-five dollars per week. Located in what is now the Wildcat Tavern, the small store sold ski apparel and equipment. These items later became staples of his own business when Reed took over the inventory of the short-lived Saks operation and opened his own store in the same location the following year.

Reed next set out to hire an instructor for the school and chose Benno Rybizka, one of Hannes Schneider's disciples in St. Anton. Rybizka, whose name, one writer noted at the time, was "easier for most Yankees to sneeze than pronounce," was a flawless skier who was also fluent in English. He had been recommended to Reed by Mary Bird, a friend and member of the 1936 U.S. Women's Ski Team who had skied with him in St. Anton. Reed wrote to Rybizka prior to the winter of 1936–37, and the Austrian ski instructor agreed to Reed's offer. The asking price for the season was $1,000 down.

INNKEEPERS CONTRIBUTE TO CAUSE

To finance the endeavor, Reed approached every innkeeper in the area from Conway to Bartlett, asking for donations of one dollar per room. "That would amount to a lot today, since the [Mount Washington] Valley has grown so much," Reed remarked in 1983. "But in those days, this town virtually hibernated in the winter and there weren't that many inns open." For their investment, the member hotels were able to offer their guests discounted lessons at the ski school.

To supplement the amount donated by innkeepers, Reed used his persuasive powers and down-to-earth integrity to convince others to contribute to the cause. "Ralph Bradley, a Boston businessman who also belonged to the White Mountain Ski Runners Club, loaned me $1,000 to get the ball rolling," Reed related.

Carroll Reed's Eastern Slope Ski School Ford Woody Wagon, or "staff car," parked in front of what is today's North Conway 5 and 10. Reed rented that space for the winter of 1938–39 before moving across the street to a cabin owned by Harvey D. Gibson, where the business expanded over the years, with Reed buying the building from Mrs. Helen Gibson in 1953. Reed later bought the old Ben Franklin store next door and connected the two buildings, according to Stefi Reed Hastings. *Courtesy of Stefi Reed Hastings.*

With the financing assured, Reed headed to New York City with two goals. One was to visit Saks Fifth Avenue's boss to discuss opening a Sak's shop in Jackson. That went well, with Saks giving Reed its OK.

The other was to meet Rybizka's boat. He was sailing from Cherbourg, France, accompanied by fellow instructor Otto Lang (1908–2006) and by Hannes Schneider (1890–1955) himself. Schneider had invited them to join him to give a demonstration of the Arlberg technique at the Boston Winter Sport Show, which had been started the year before as America's first ski show in Boston Garden, and then to appear at the show at Madison Square Garden, according to Lang in his 1994 book, *A Bird of Passage*. Together, the two shows drew 200,000 spectators, according to Lang. They arrived in New York, and without overnighting, they took an express train to Boston, followed by the show in New York.

Reed said it was all good publicity for his new ski school. "Of course, I tried to get them [Schneider, Lang and Rybizka] to tell about the fact that there'd be a new ski school in [Jackson]. And that happened to be the same year that Sun Valley opened, the same year that Sepp Ruschp had his ski school [in Stowe, Vermont]. So we all opened together," Reed said in a January 1991 interview furnished by his daughter, Stefi Reed Hastings.

After the shows, Schneider sailed back to Europe. Rybizka headed for Jackson to start the season for Reed's new Eastern Slope Ski School, and Lang traveled west to Mount Rainier to found his branch of the Schneider school.

Reed Meets Mr. Gibson

For his trip to New York to meet up with the Saks people, Reed was advised by Dr. Harold Shedd of the Eastern Slope Ski Club to pay a courtesy call while there at the Manufacturers Trust Company to its president, Harvey D. Gibson, a former Fryeburg Academy classmate of Shedd's, North Conway native and part-time resident.

Reed later related that the meeting went well, as Gibson seemed pleased to hear of the endeavor and what Reed envisioned it could do for the economy of Gibson's hometown—and also that he was not there to seek any money from the banker. It was the first of many future meetings.

"He listened to my plan for holding ski classes in Jackson that winter, then leaned forward and asked to know what I desired of him," said Reed. "When I told him that I only wanted to let him know of my plans, he smiled, leaned back in his chair, and we spoke for an hour."

RYBIZKA ARRIVES

After the Boston and New York ski shows, Rybizka (1904–1992) arrived in Jackson in December 1936. With barely ten days to prepare for the opening of the ski school, the precise, Austrian "drillmaster" set about teaching a group of local boys not only how to instruct but also how to ski.

Compounding the problem was the fact that the winter of 1936–37 proved to be almost snowless. Even worse, whenever it did snow, rain followed. Looking back on those first weeks of organized skiing in Jackson, Rybizka noted that times were trying at best.

"I soon began to realize that I was confronted with most serious problems. First of all, no slopes. Second, the boys I met seemed interested but alas were poor skiers and last, but not least, there was no snow to start training. Had I known at that time that we also had to face a winter without snow, I probably would have thrown in the towel," recalled Rybizka in his paper, "The History of the Eastern Slope Ski School."

Rybizka had asked Reed to round up some local boys to serve as instructors—not necessarily skiers but "clean-cut youths" who were also good athletes. Reed turned first to the town hockey team, recruiting J. Arthur Doucette and Arthur Callan. Tyler Micoleau, a local artist, ran into Reed one day in the post office, and since the two had previously met on the ski slopes, he was asked to join the crew. Francis Savard, who worked in his father's meat market, was also invited to instruct.

Others who enlisted that first year included 1936 Olympian Mary Bird, Bob Morrell (later co-founder of Story Land after the war), Hugh and Chet Emerson, Bill Duprey and Clarke Edwards.

"Time was short before the official opening of the ski school," Rybizka noted, "neither did it snow and realizing all that, I concentrated on teaching the fundamentals of skiing on what was at hand and that was Whitneys' slope—we had nothing else…When the last lesson was over, I asked the boys to do some freestyle skiing down that hill. Not one made it without a fall."

SKIING ON…FROZEN SHEEP MANURE?

When even the patches of snow at Whitneys' proved inadequate, Rybizka moved the classes to the smooth slopes at the ninth hole of the Eagle Mountain House golf course above Jackson Village. "It was a blessing that

Married in 1937, Carroll and Kay (Damon) Reed were a great husband-and-wife business team at Carroll Reed Ski Shops. They raised three daughters and gave tirelessly to the community. They sold the business in 1969. Carroll was one of the founders of the Conway Scenic Railroad in 1974. *Courtesy of Stefi Reed Hastings.*

we did not know we would have to stay there the rest of the winter, but that we did," wrote Rybizka. "We did have several snow falls that winter, but alas every one of them was followed by a thaw and rain. I almost still hear myself groan when I heard the water dripping off the roof of Jimmy Amstels [*sic*] hotel: 'Good God, not again!'"

"We literally skied on the combination of light snow and sheep manure that winter," Reed agreed in an interview, noting that the golf course had been organically fertilized by local flocks of sheep prior to the start of the season. "Combined with the light snow," he laughed, "it provided an adequate cover for skiing."

A perfectionist at heart, Rybizka was a firm follower of Schneider's Arlberg technique, which required that skiers master the simplest of steps before advancing to more difficult skills. As Rybizka wrote in his 1939 book, *The Hannes Schneider Ski Technique*:

> *Hannes Schneider came to St. Anton in 1907. He used an entirely new technique in skiing, different from the Norwegian ski technique, and also distinctive from the Zdarsky technique by reason of its speed. Forward leaning, outside leaning, and the low crouch were the characteristics of this new technique—the Arlberg technique—which was used by the young skiers at this time, but none of them except Hannes Schneider tried to explain or teach it. He never claimed to have invented this technique, but he rightfully* [claimed] *that he was the first and only skier who tried to find out its principles, define them and understand them, and reduce them to their simplest and most logical maneuvers for teaching purposes.*

The Arlberg technique emphasized leaning forward and bending the knees, swinging the hips and shoulders and stemming in an up-and-down movement on the turn. When skiers mastered the snowplow, they would move onto the stem turn and then to the stem christiana and, finally, the parallel turn, in that order. "He [Hannes] tried to analyze all those complicated maneuvers in skiing and to teach them step by step to the beginners so logically and simply that no one would fail to learn how," wrote Rybizka in his book.

His strict adherence did not win him any popularity contests at the time. "Benno was awfully strong on that snowplow turn. We all called it 'snowplow-itis.' He'd hold people back until they could do it well," Reed noted.

With characteristic humor, Dick May, one of the first pupils that year, in a 1986 interview added, "With Benno, when you were able to do a snowplow turn pretty well, you just moved up to do it on a steeper slope. By the time you got through, you could practically do linked snowplow turns over the [Tuckerman Ravine] headwall."

After a few days out on the slopes, Rybizka opted to hold a series of après-ski fireside chats at Reed's Saks Ski Shop office to give them pointers. "That was the only chance I had to improve their teaching and also in some way their skiing," Rybizka noted.

In spite of the poor ski season, Reed's Eastern Slope Ski School (Headquarters/Carroll Reed/ESSS/American Branch/Hannes Schneider's Ski School/St. Anton am Arlberg, Austria/Benno Rybizka/Ski Master) gave six thousand lessons that first winter, with instructors and students skiing some days in raincoats. Innkeepers noted that what normally would have been a disastrous season turned out better than they had hoped; the fascination of the ski classes held the winter visitors in the mountains even without the snow.

"People came from Boston, Providence, Portland, Manchester and Concord and they stayed in inns up and down the Valley," Reed recalled in an interview for the *Jackson Skiing Legends* commemorative booklet published in 1986 on the fiftieth anniversary of the founding of the school and written by Karen Cummings. "We were amazed at the publicity we got and the response from all the people."

Rybizka credited his instructors for a lot of that success. "In spite of all the most adverse weather conditions during that entire winter, the ski school was a success. But great credit should be given to the local boys who acted as instructors and only their spirit and enthusiasm made that success possible," Rybizka said.

Snow finally did come that first ski school winter of 1936–37 on Washington's birthday, too late to be of much use for attracting the big crowds, but the season did continue all the way to April 11.

So happy were the innkeepers whose rooms had been filled with the burgeoning number of ski students that they agreed to Reed's plan to send the local instructors to Austria that spring for further schooling in the Alps under Rybizka. The entire valley contributed to the effort by holding various raffles and fundraisers. Edna Ricker of Kearsarge Hall even auctioned off a pig. Reed—as president and owner of the ski school—personally paid for half the trip himself and also loaned each of his instructors $100 in cash. Taking the trip were Callan, Savard, Doucette, Micoleau, John "Jake" May and Bert Jensen of Hanover, who joined the group at his own expense.

While in St. Anton, the boys were put to the ultimate test and met the challenge head-on. "At the end of May it so happened that the Austrian

Carroll Reed (center) for nearly forty years operated a branch of his ski shop at Mount Cranmore. Helping Reed take stock of his Cranmore shop's inventory in the late 1940s were Cliff Smith (left) and Herbert Schneider (right). *Courtesy of North Conway Public Library.*

State Ski Examination took place at St. Christoph and I asked the examiners to test the teaching and skiing abilities of the American instructors. They obliged, and all the boys passed with flying colors," Rybizka said.

Gibsons Visit Jackson

When skier and future Hollywood actress Whitney Bourne, Harvey Gibson's stepdaughter, came to Jackson in January 1937 to take a lesson at Reed's school, Gibson came along to watch. Being a man of vision and a loyal supporter of North Conway, Gibson got to thinking: if Jackson could be a ski resort then so could his hometown of North Conway. But more on that in the next chapter. Plans began to grow in Gibson's ever-entrepreneurial mind.

Buying Cranmore Mountain in North Conway three weeks later, Gibson set out to transform North Conway into a ski resort. He prevailed upon Reed to move his rope tow to Cranmore from Thorn Mountain in Jackson, allowing Reed to retain ownership while he paid for the cost of moving it. The lift hauled skiers at Cranmore during the winter of 1937–38—Cranmore's first season with tow service—with skiing offered on the South Slope.

A front-page story in the *Reporter* of January 27, 1938, carried the headline "Cranmore Slope Enlarged." Noted the story:

> *Men began clearing additional slopes on Cranmore Mountain Monday as the preliminary step of a $5,000* [Works Progress Administration] *project to increase Eastern Slope ski facilities. The slope developed this year by the local Chamber of Commerce, where Carroll Reed recently installed a 1,000-foot ski tow, will be lengthened until it reaches nearly to the top of 1,700-foot mountain. A trail continues from the top of the present slopes for about three hundred yards through a heavy growth of pine. Tentative plans are to clear the hardwood above the strip of pine with the government money, and subsequently sell the standing pine. The result will be a slope nearly a mile long with considerable variations in grade. The new area will not be completed in time for skiing this winter, but will be a valuable supplement to regional facilities another year.*

To complement the development of the ski area, Gibson had bought the Hotel Randall in North Conway in the summer of 1937 and renamed it the Eastern Slope Inn. An outlet of the Carroll Reed Ski Shop of Jackson opened in the inn that fall, while a branch of the Eastern Slope Ski School was established at Mount Cranmore.

Meanwhile, Bill and Betty Whitney were developing Whitneys' into a major area in Jackson, with Bill adapting the area's 1935-built overhead cable lift by adding seventy-two Sears Roebuck shovel handles, onto which skiers hung as they were pulled up the mountain. The summer of '37 also saw the town of Jackson building ski trails under local ski instructor Arthur Doucette's direction, with the town appropriating $2,000 for that purpose.

Twelve Thousand Lessons Given

Rybizka returned from Europe to run the ski school that second season in 1937–38, directing the new branch at the newly opened Cranmore while fellow St. Anton am Arlberg instructor Franz Koessler ran the Jackson branch. More local instructors joined the schools, and with more snow, the winter proved a success, with twelve thousand lessons given at the two branches of the school.

Skiing in the Eastern Slope Region was developing at a rapid rate by that second winter. A ski slope was cleared on the West Side at Birch Hill, offering more terrain, and then Cranmore took a giant step when Gibson hired local inventor George Morton to build the lower Skimobile. Work commenced on the contraption during the summer of '38.

Rybizka and Gibson talked that summer of '38 about the possibility of obtaining the release of skimeister Hannes Schneider from Nazi custody and bringing him to Mount Cranmore. Schneider had been arrested in Austria for his anti-Nazi views in March 1938 and held under house arrest in Germany. Various European resorts had made overtures to Schneider to take over their operations, but Gibson persevered in his attempts to bring him to North Conway.

As part of the plan, Gibson made an offer to purchase Reed's ski school so that he could, in turn, offer the school to Schneider. Gibson bought stock in the school, paying Reed $25 a week for five years, totaling $3,000, freeing Reed to concentrate his efforts on his growing ski shop and clothing business.

Reed recalled that Gibson's offer to buy the ski school took him by surprise and initially troubled him but notes he soon realized that selling the school to the influential banker made sense for the community. "Selling the ski school wasn't my idea, as it was proposed to me at a club meeting that summer by [Eastern Slope Ski Club directors] Dr. Shedd, Noel Wellman and Joe Dodge. It was a blow to me at first, but then, after considering it, I realized that it was absolutely the best for the community. And Mr. Gibson was a great guy to do business with," Reed noted, adding, "One reason Dr. Shedd and Mr. Wellman wanted me to sell the school was because I couldn't run it with Benno. Benno was so rigid—there was no give to him. Just as he said, is just what he wanted. They wanted me to sell the school and let it be owned by the community, so they could have Hannes [Schneider, once he was released from captivity] run it, but I knew that wouldn't be practical. I knew that Mr. Gibson was negotiating for Hannes Schneider's release, and that's why I sold it to him. I knew it would be good for the community. He paid me a few thousand dollars in assets," said Reed.

Just as it had under Reed's ownership, the two ski schools continued to grow under Gibson's control that second season for Cranmore and the third year for the ski school in the winter of '38–39. The staffs of the schools increased to twenty instructors that season, with two more Schneider disciples—nineteen-year-old ski sensation Toni Matt and Otto Tschol—quietly leaving Austria with Koessler to join Rybizka at the respective schools in Jackson and North Conway.

"Franz, Toni and I snuck out before the Nazis knew it and we set sail from Bremerhaven [Germany]. We weren't allowed to take more than 10 shillings out of the country, which was a problem, because you had to have $50 to be allowed into America. But Mr. Gibson took care of that," recalled Tschol in a 1988 interview.

When the trio arrived in New York Harbor, Gibson sent one of his emissaries out in a police launch to greet them and slipped them fifty dollars each. "Of course," Tschol added, "we had to pay him back later."

Snow trains—which first began coming to New Hampshire from the cities in 1931—grew in popularity. The first came to North Conway in 1932. Once Cranmore opened in 1937–38, skiers flocked to North Conway to learn how to ski at Cranmore and other local slopes.

Meanwhile, negotiations for Schneider's release continued, unbeknownst to those skiers, and if anyone had ever doubted Harvey Dow Gibson's persuasive powers, they shouldn't have. Using his influence as a member of the board that oversaw Germany's credit, Gibson made an offer to Germany's finance minister: release Schneider and his family and Germany's short-term credit would be extended.

The Skimeister Arrives

The Nazis accepted the offer, and Schneider was released. Arriving in North Conway on February 11, 1939, the Schneiders were quickly welcomed into the community. Hannes Schneider was named director of the ski school now owned by Gibson, and he was also named honorary president of the Eastern Slope Ski Club.

Reed noted that he was happy to see Schneider take over the school because of the prestige he brought to the region. "Hannes did bring in a lot of upper crust to North Conway, and they were quite proud to say they'd taken lessons from him before in Europe. His presence did make a difference, and with Harvey Gibson's 'Ski Lark' snow train, a lot of influential folks from New York began coming up," said Reed.

It did bother Reed, however, when the school's Jackson branch was discontinued during the latter part of World War II, when gas rationing made driving to Jackson a prohibitive journey. Cranmore boomed during the war years because it was located near the rail lines, but Jackson was too remote. "Because the original purpose of the school was to serve all of the valley, I didn't like the way they had to stop the school in Jackson, but with no gas, and the closest rail service only to Glen, it didn't make sense," Reed related to this reporter in 1983.

As for Rybizka, he later moved on to open ski schools in Mitterill, Lake Placid, Mont Tremblant and Portillo, Chile. He returned to Austria in 1953 to care for his elderly stepmother.

Carroll and Kay Reed, Partners

With the capital from the sale of the ski school, Carroll and Kay Reed addressed their attention to their growing retail business. They operated from the Eastern Slope Inn, moved to the North Conway 5 Cent to $1.00 Store on Main Street and later relocated in a small cabin across Main Street. Gibson owned the building.

"He asked me why I didn't rent that building and I told him Mr. Gibson, I could never afford that," Reed related while giving a reporter a history-minded tour of North Conway in 1983. "He patted me on the shoulder, and said, 'Carroll, let me worry about that.' We didn't pay rent for the first five years," said Reed, still awed years later by Gibson's generosity and civic-mindedness.

They soon enlarged the building and installed wood stoves to heat it.

The Reeds produced their first mail-order catalogue in the fall of 1939 and worked together with their staff over the ensuing years to make the business a leader in the clothing and sporting goods field. Their fifty shops were located throughout the ski country of New Hampshire. In 1966–67, Kay and Carroll were named "Ski Retailers of the Year" by Ski Industries of America.

Carroll Reed (right) is shown having a conversation with Hannes Schneider (left) at a cocktail party at the Reeds' home in Kearsarge in 1945. The Reeds were active in business and civic affairs in the community. *Courtesy of Stefi Reed Hastings.*

Active Ski Community

The Reeds had three daughters: Carol Reed Karnopp, who died in 1985 in a plane crash; Damon "Pokey" Reed; and Stefi (Reed Markham) Hastings.

Damon and Stefi in 2012 recalled their parents as being part of a social network that revolved around skiing. "Friends were always dropping by," said Hastings, adding that dinner parties were frequent, as were après-ski visits to the Slalom Lounge at the Oxen Yoke run by the Ostermaiers.

Among those who were shop (and often house) visitors was Howard Head of Head Skis and later Head metal tennis racquets fame. Norwegian 1952 Oslo Olympic gold medalist Stein Eriksen—said to be skiing's first superstar for his aerial feats—was a houseguest early in the 1950s. Others who socialized at the Reeds' house near the four corners in Kearsarge included Harvey and Helen Gibson and skiwear company founder Klaus Obermeyer—Carroll Reed's was his first turtleneck customer, according to Hastings.

Things got especially busy around the time of the Gibson Trophy Cup Races, held at Cranmore every year from 1940 to 1966. "During the Gibson weekend, we'd have a whole assortment of racers for cocktails or whatever," recalled Hastings in a 2012 interview, noting that her mother, Kay, was "always the head of gatekeepers…Each gate had two gatekeepers…who were well supplied with drink during the race."

The list of multi-Gibson winners includes such names as Paula Kann (Valar), Toni Matt, Edi Mall and Ann Johnson Jones. Other winners and guests included Leona Reny (now Hill) and 1956 Olympian and 1960 Olympic two-time silver medalist Penny Pitou.

The Reeds in Business

Carroll Reed, in a 1983 interview with this writer, stressed that he always put customer service at the top of his list. "Harvey Gibson always told me that if you take care of the customers, they'll take care of you," said Reed, a message he conveyed to his employees. "I always told my employees that they worked for our customers and not for me. We stressed integrity and quality," he added, "and it paid off."

Getting the Carroll Reed's Treatment

In a fall 2012 interview, former Cranmore ski patrol member, longtime snowsports adult school supervisor and Cranmore Snowsports Hall of Fame founder Donnie Newton, sixty-five, of Conway shared his personal favorite Carroll Reed story. "My parents were divorced when I was young, so my mom was a single parent raising my sister and me. We didn't have a lot of money, and like many local kids, thank God for the Eastern Slope Ski Club Junior Program, because that's how we learned to ski," he said.

He said a lot of his early ski technique was taught on a snowy slope behind his River Street home in Conway. His neighbor and instructor was Bob Morrell (1920–1998), one of the original local Eastern Slope Ski School instructors, a former ESSC Junior Program coordinator and a past Carroll Reed's Shop employee who in 1954 co-founded Story Land with his wife, Ruth. He taught their daughter, Nancy Morrell, and the Newton kids how to ski at the small neighborhood slope and also made it possible for the Newtons to be able to ski at Cranmore.

When Newton was thirteen, it was time for a new pair of skis. His parents separately gave what they could round up, which was a combined total of seventy dollars—not enough for new equipment. On a Friday night, the junior high student consequently walked past the newer skis, Bogner stretch pants and Icelandic sweaters on display on the first floor of Carroll Reed's and proceeded directly to the basement level, where he knew that used and rental equipment was sold. He spied a pair of Kneissl Combi Ws with bindings on the rack. They were beauties, but looking at the tag, he saw that they cost ninety dollars—half the price of a new pair from upstairs but too much for his budget. Just then, he heard a man's voice.

"Can I help you, young man?" said the voice.

Newton looked up to see that the voice belonged to Carroll Reed himself, who was manning the basement counter that night and wearing a leather sales apron.

"I'm looking to get a pair of new skis and bindings. I've looked around. I really like these Kneissls, but they're way too expensive for me," said young Newton.

"Just how much do you have?" asked Reed.

Newton said he looked into his wallet and counted it up. "Seventy dollars," he told Reed.

With that, Reed took a felt-tipped pen out of his apron pocket and crossed out the ninety-dollar mark on the tag, replacing it with a new figure: "Seventy dollars. Enjoy your skis," Newton says Reed told him.

"That was Carroll Reed!" said Newton in October 2012 about that night from fifty-two years ago.

Appropriately enough, the interview took place at the Frontside Grind, across from what was once Reed's and for several years has been home to

1952 and '56 Olympian Brooks Dodge (left) is shown with Carroll P. Reed, Mrs. Helen Gibson and Herta Schneider Fahrner in this photo from the early 1960s. *Courtesy of Stefi Reed Hastings.*

Olympia Sports. The Frontside is located in the former Lyman's Shell gas station—like Reed's, a former village landmark. Reed's is gone, but the landmark "world's tallest ski pole" remains on the sidewalk in front of what was once Reed's.

CIVIC VOLUNTEERS

Never ones to shirk civic duties, Carroll and Kay spent half of their time overseeing their business and raising their three daughters and the rest of their hours helping out the community. Both were active in the Eastern Slope Ski Club and also with Memorial Hospital. Kay served on the Conway School Board as well.

Just as Harvey Dow Gibson had helped him out when he first got started, Reed noted he felt an obligation to help his community in whatever way he could. "We were never too busy to talk with someone or to serve on anything that was beneficial to the community," Reed said, noting that "anyone worth his salt" would do the same. "That commitment to a community spirit is what's always made this area so special and such a pleasant place to work for Kay and I," he said in 1988.

After working long and hard to nurture their business, the Reeds sold their store in October 1969. At the age of sixty-five, Carroll said it was time for him to step down and let someone else take the reins of the growing company. "I'm a believer in the Peter Principle—everyone has a certain optimum capacity, and we'd reached ours," he explained.

Reed later became involved with such ventures as the restoration of the North Conway Train Station and the operation of the Conway Scenic Railroad, which was founded in 1974 with partner Bill Levy of Yield House and the Maine Central Railroad's Dwight Smith.

By 1985, Carroll Reed's was owned by Charles M. Leighton of CML Group, who sold it to Swire Pacific in 1990. It was later purchased by D.M. Management, which became J. Jill Group, which shut it down in 1996.

The Reeds' business legacy is carried on by many who worked for them—including Stan Millen and Dan Lewis of Stan & Dan's Sports of North Conway, both of whom were employed at Carroll Reed's in its heyday and continue its dedication to customer service and quality ski goods. The shop is a multi–*Ski Magazine* Gold Medal Winner in yearly readers' polls.

Some people are able to turn misfortune into opportunity. Carroll Reed was among them, aided staunchly by Kay, his business and life partner. Downed by a broken back, he overcame his disability and founded a ski school so others could learn to ski properly. That school, in turn, benefited the local economy, just as Reed had envisioned. Their store proved to be a regional success, built on their high standards.

"It seems like everything fell into place for me," Reed, ever humble, explained in 1988, noting he has always been a strong believer in fate. "I've always felt like I could look to the guy upstairs for direction."

Carroll died in January 1995, and Kay passed away in June 1999. Because of their lifelong commitment to serving the community, the Reeds will always be part of the valley's ski history.

CHAPTER 4

HARVEY D. GIBSON

BANKING ON THE MOUNTAINS

New York City bank president. World financier. Chairman of the American Red Cross during World Wars I and II. Chairman of the American Committee of Short-Term Creditors of Germany. President of the New York World's Fair in 1940. A man of extraordinary intellect, energy and vision, Cranmore founder Harvey Dow Gibson was all of those things and more. Larger than life in the nation and world's business and political community, he was a native son of North Conway who never forgot his hometown.

Gibson literally banked on the mountains, doing what he could to improve the year-round economic base of the region—and skiing became a key part of that plan.

TIRELESS ENERGY

Looking over his many accomplishments, one questions just how Gibson was able to achieve so much in his sixty-eight years. Some of the answers may be found in his autobiography, *Harvey Dow Gibson*, published by his widow Helen Whitney Gibson (1890–1970) in 1951.

Harvey Dow Gibson (1882–1950) was an influential New York City businessman and political insider who was born and raised in North Conway. Gibson acquired Mount Cranmore in 1937 and developed it for skiing, seeing it as a way to improve the region's winter economy. Cranmore opened for its first season of lift-serviced skiing with a rope tow in January 1938. *Courtesy of North Conway Public Library.*

Other insights come from those who knew Gibson, with many recalling him as a generous and buoyant man, full of energy and life. "Harvey was a great guy, with a lot of bounce and life to him," recalled the late Kay Damon Reed (1916–1999) of Kearsarge, partners with her husband, Carroll P. Reed, in the region's classic apparel Carroll Reed's retailing shops. Carroll Reed founded the region's first ski school in Jackson in December 1936, which eventually led to Gibson's getting involved in the ski business himself.

In a 1988 interview, Kay Reed related how helpful Gibson had been to them, as well as how amazed she was at how much Gibson was able to accomplish in his life. "I remember asking Harvey once how he was able to do so much," Kay related, "and he just said, 'Kay, I'll tell ya: I make up my mind very quickly. You find your batting average is pretty good if you don't dawdle.'"

JUST WHO WAS GIBSON?

Gibson's life, from all appearances, was an embodiment of the American dream, built out of a strict work ethic. Born in North Conway on March 12, 1882, the son of a railroad station agent who later owned a lumber business, Gibson attended Fryeburg Academy and graduated from Bowdoin College in 1902.

His first contact with the business world upon his graduation was with the American Express Company in Boston, where he swept out the office and served as a courier. Although discouraged and contemplating quitting, young Gibson chose to stick it out, a decision that proved to be the first of many good turns of fortune in his successful career, according to his autobiography.

After paying his dues, Gibson left his janitorial duties behind and soon worked his way up to a number of assistant posts in the company. When American Express's financial manager in Montreal suffered a nervous breakdown, Gibson was named as a replacement in 1905. Success there resulted in his return to Boston as an assistant manager, a post he soon left to strike out in business on his own as the co-owner of a successful travel agency.

Two years later, he was asked by the new president of New York's Liberty National Bank to be his assistant. When that official joined J.P. Morgan's firm in 1916, thirty-four-year-old Harvey Gibson was chosen as

Son of a station agent, Harvey Dow Gibson was born on March 12, 1882, and raised in this home on Artist Falls Road in North Conway. After paying his dues in the business world, he won his spurs in financial circles by being named New York City's youngest bank president at the age of thirty-four in 1916. He went on to serve in several posts, including as director of the Red Cross in Europe in World War I and on the Committee for Germany's Short-Term Debt. *Courtesy of North Conway Public Library.*

his successor. He soon won his spurs in the New York financial district as the city's youngest bank president.

His promotion occurred just fourteen and a half years after he had landed his first job at American Express, and it symbolized the start of what, from then on, would be an influential and far-reaching career.

International Service

When the United States entered World War I, Gibson served as general manager of the American Red Cross in 1917 and Red Cross commissioner of France in 1918 and for all of Europe in 1919. In recognition of his service, he was awarded the Legion of Honor by the French government and returned home after the war to resume directorship of the Liberty National Bank.

He left the Morgan Bank in 1930 to resuscitate the Manufacturers Trust Company, attaining some notoriety in financial circles by being one of only six men whom J.P. Morgan ever called on in their own offices.

Harvey Dow Gibson stands at the base of Cranmore reading a copy of the *Saturday Evening Post* that carried a story on New Hampshire skiing called "Poor Man's Snow Heaven." Note the poster in the foreground. *Courtesy of New England Ski Museum.*

The Depression Descends

Trouble was brewing worldwide at the time of Gibson's appointment at Manufacturers. Unemployment across the country was growing at an alarming rate, affecting millions in New York City alone. Up to that time, no forms of unemployment insurance existed, the Works Progress Administration had yet to be formed and there was no state or federal aid available to cope with the situation.

A citizens' committee, composed of leaders from all walks of life, was formed to raise $5 million for the unemployed workers of New York City. That fundraising goal was met, but due to the enormity of the problem, the funds were soon depleted.

Harvey Gibson was named to serve as chairman of the committee for a second appeal in the summer of 1931. The group succeeded in raising an additional $20 million, exceeding its own expectations. When the conditions worsened the following summer, Gibson once again organized a third relief drive, which raised another $15 million.

Economic woes continued to worsen during the summer of 1931. Many banks closed their doors, depositors became alarmed about the security of their savings and bank runs began to occur more frequently as the year progressed. Assets of banks could not be liquidated rapidly enough to keep pace with the withdrawal of deposits.

The peak of the bank closings occurred the week before President Franklin Roosevelt was inaugurated on March 4, 1933. Roosevelt declared a bank holiday as one of his first official acts in an attempt to alleviate the bleak economic situation.

Skiing Develops in the 1930s

Meanwhile, as the rest of the country was experiencing economic hard times and Harvey Gibson was steering his company through its consequent difficulties, the sport of skiing was growing in popularity in the White Mountains. Early pioneers of the sport confined their activities for the most part to Tuckerman Ravine on the eastern side of Mount Washington, but as skiing grew, the undeveloped hills of mountain villages such as Jackson and Gorham attracted their share of winter enthusiasts.

Influential in international finance, Harvey Gibson was a man of many interests. During the Great Depression, he served President Franklin Roosevelt, helping to chair relief drives for the unemployed. Here he is shown with First Lady Eleanor Roosevelt. *Courtesy of North Conway Public Library.*

Harvey Gibson was not the instigator of the movement to develop the Eastern Slope Region as a ski resort, but he soon was in touch with one of those individuals who was at the forefront: Carroll Reed.

SKIING AS AN ECONOMIC BOOST

As a result of Reed's paying a courtesy call in New York in December 1936 to North Conway's most famous and influential native son, Gibson's interest in skiing was sparked. It was heightened a month later while accompanying his stepdaughter Whitney Bourne on a visit to Jackson in January 1937. He says he assumed that Whitney (later an actress) would be spending time with her mother and Gibson over New Year's in North Conway, but she was intent on trying her hand at skiing. So, to Whitneys' in Jackson they drove.

"At that time," wrote Gibson in his autobiography, "there were no facilities in North Conway, and those supposed to be the authorities on skiing and the best judges of the most desirable slopes and trails, did not consider that there were any that could be developed in North Conway comparable to Jackson." Gibson—being a true and loyal North Conwayite—wondered if North Conway might not be able to provide even better skiing than Jackson.

While admitting that he knew little about the sport, Gibson refused to give up his notion. "I most emphatically could not see why North Conway shouldn't be the ski center of the region," wrote Gibson. "True, I knew practically nothing about skiing, but I loved North Conway so much that I could not believe that there was anything in which it could not excel if it went about it in the right way."

Turning the idea over, Gibson's thoughts focused on the area at the base of Lookout Point on Mount Cranmore. Gibson visited the mountain and carefully inspected it for its skiing potential. Judging those possibilities to be strong, he wrote that he "acted on impulse and quietly acquired most of the west side of Cranmore Mountain" in January 1937.

He announced to the North Conway Chamber of Commerce in March of that year that he planned to develop it into a ski area, according to a booklet, *History of the Eastern Slope Ski Club, 1936–2006*. The ESSC was asked

Opening day at Cranmore, January 1938. The area was serviced by a rope tow that first season, moved by Carroll Reed at Harvey D. Gibson's request from Jackson. *Tom Eastman collection.*

to appoint a committee to work with the chamber of commerce to make recommendations for the development, the booklet noted. Immediate plans included the clearing of trees, doing so with the help of Works Progress Administration grants.

Gibson next carried his plan to turn North Conway into a ski center further by negotiating to purchase the Hotel Randall in August 1937. Renaming the 1926-built Colonial-style structure the Eastern Slope Inn to tie in with the efforts being made to promote the region, Gibson announced that the hotel would be operated on a year-round basis, with steps taken to promote the inn as a center for winter sports enthusiasts.

For the first season of Cranmore in 1937–38, Gibson paid Reed to move a rope tow from Thorn Mountain in Jackson that had never been used the year before during the first snow-challenged season of Reed's ski school. He also invited Reed to open a second branch of his ski school at Cranmore. He offered office space at the hotel in fall 1937 to the ESSC, with Kay Damon (later Reed) serving as its first paid secretary.

MORTON'S SKIMOBILE

Next, Gibson set his sights on the installation of a ski lift of some sort. All overhead cable ski lifts with J-Bar hangers at the time were patented by a Swiss inventor named Victor Constam, and Gibson, as the story goes, didn't want to pay royalties.

Undaunted, Gibson followed the advice of his friend W. Averell Harriman (1891–1986), developer of the Sun Valley ski area, which had opened with the world's first two chairlifts in 1936. Gibson proceeded with his plans to build a ski lift of an altogether new design.

Hired as an engineer for the Cranmore job was Goodrich Falls mechanic, engineer and inventor George Morton.

CHAPTER 5
THE EASTERN SLOPE INN
HARVEY D. GIBSON'S IN-TOWN HOTEL

Now owned separately by avid master ski racer and ski history enthusiast Joe Berry of Eastern Slope Inn Associates, the Eastern Slope Inn has long had a close connection to Cranmore Mountain Resort. Just as his friend and wealthy, influential colleague W. Averell Harriman of New York built the Sun Valley Lodge in Idaho as part of his overall development of skiing there in 1936, original Cranmore owner Harvey Dow Gibson knew that he needed a resort hotel to go hand in hand with his plans to develop local winter and summer tourism in North Conway. In the summer of 1937, Gibson filled that need by acquiring the former Hotel Randall, which he renamed the Eastern Slope Inn.

RICH HISTORY

In 1926, hotelier Henry Harrison "Harry" Randall built the third Hotel Randall to be located on the site. Like so many White Mountain stick-built resort hotels, the two previous Hotel Randalls were consumed by fire.

Randall's father, James Thompson Randall, had given up shopkeeping and bought a boardinghouse on the north end of Main Street in 1854, renaming

Just as Sun Valley had the Sun Valley Lodge when it opened in 1936, Cranmore developer Harvey Dow Gibson knew he needed an in-town hotel to serve the needs of skiers. After buying the undeveloped mountain in January 1937, Gibson bought the Hotel Randall in the summer of 1937. He renamed it the Eastern Slope Inn (pictured here), announcing that it would undergo renovations and would thereafter be open on a year-round basis. *Courtesy of North Conway Public Library.*

it the Hotel Randall. Harry Randall was born in 1870, four years before the arrival of the railroad to town, and he grew up working in various capacities at his family's hotel, which was enlarged over the years. It burned to the ground on November 19, 1902. Undaunted by the disaster, Harry—who had assumed ownership upon his father's death in 1898—began to rebuild, and the second "New" Hotel Randall opened on the same site on July 6, 1903.

Built in the popular Dutch Colonial style with a mansard roof, the Hotel Randall grew quickly. In 1916, an addition brought the room total to fifty—thirty-three of which had private baths. A brochure boasted that the inn had all the latest amenities, including "telephones, electric bells, electric lights, and steam heat." Expansion continued in 1917 with the purchase of the adjacent Sunset Pavilion, a popular summer hotel located between the present-day hotel and what is now the Eastern Slope Playhouse.

The second Hotel Randall was a year-round resort, and although North Conway was better known as a summer destination, it was rapidly gaining popularity as a winter resort. Sledding and tobogganing behind the hotel were popular, as was a snowshoeing trek behind the inn into the woods to enjoy coffee and hot doughnuts served around a campfire. Skating, sled dog racing and the beginnings of skiing were also attracting larger numbers of winter vacationers to the area, and the Randall House with its luxury appointments and central location was among the most fashionable places to stay. The hotel's popularity prompted another expansion in 1921. An entire wing was added, bringing the capacity of the hotel to 150 guests.

The economy was strong, and the region's hotels prospered. But tragedy struck again on November 20, 1925, when fire consumed the inn in less than three hours, almost twenty-three years to the day of the first fire. Construction on the third Hotel Randall began in less than a month, with the new hotel opening in July 1926. It is that hotel that survives to this day.

A front-page article in the July 1, 1926 *North Conway Reporter* saluted the Randalls for having "gone ahead with reckless courage and erected the most up-to-date and modern, if not the finest, hotel in New Hampshire, a distinct credit to the town, country, and state." The new hotel was as fireproof as possible, with fire stops in every wall, cement floors in the kitchen and basement, boilers outside the building, wiring in protective cable and a sprinkler system throughout.

Just three years after the grand opening of the hotel with a gala ball, things took a turn for the Randalls, the hotel and the country with the crash of the stock market, ushering in the Great Depression. Vacationing as a way of life changed dramatically, with luxurious getaways among the first to go. With the advent of the automobile, travel modes changed as well, with guest cabins and later motels replacing the grand hotels.

Harry Randall and his sons held on, but the die was cast. Harry mortgaged the place to such an extent that he was essentially managing the place for the banks.

Gibson Buys Hotel

Harvey Gibson needed a hotel for his resort plans; Randall and the banks needed cash. Gibson bought then-undeveloped Cranmore in January 1937 and then acquired the inn in summer 1937. He renamed it the Eastern Slope Inn and announced it would be open for year-round business.

The ground floor was extensively remodeled for the reopening, and a large après-ski room was added to the southwest corner of the building. Said the *Reporter*, "It is bound to be one of the most popular rooms in the house, with its walls decorated with life-size pictures of the Currier & Ives type"—hence the name that would become known to skiers for years to come, the Currier & Ives Room.

The article continued to describe the room by noting, "Just to the north is a small but attractive grill, whose walls depict gaily colored elephants in ski scenes."

The inn reopened in December 1937, in time for the start of Cranmore's first lift-serviced season. The inn became the focal point of après-ski life in the village during Gibson's ownership.

Former chair of the 1939 and 1940 New York World's Fair, Gibson brought the Swiss Orchestra to North Conway to become the house band after the fair. Ever full of life, whether in financial endeavors or music, he often sat in on mandolin with the Swiss Orchestra.

THE AUSTRIAN CONNECTION

Austrian instructors congregated there after ski hours, especially after Gibson won skimeister Hannes Schneider's release from Nazi custody in February 1939. The Schneiders were regulars in the dining room as part of Hannes Schneider's contract with Gibson.

"We would eat breakfast, lunch and dinner at the inn. It was very, very nice," said Herbert Schneider in 2008, then eighty-eight and still living in the house that Gibson obtained for the Schneider family prior to their arrival in February 1939, just down the street from Cranmore and the inn. That house is now occupied by the younger of the late Doris and Herbert Schneider's two sons, Christoph.

"We would come down for lunch from the mountain, dining at 12:30 p.m.," recalled Herbert. "Father would always go into the lounge and enjoy a martini. Then, we would go back to teach afternoon lessons at the ski school. For a time, the inn had a ski-and-stay package, which allowed everyone to ski for free if they stayed at the inn. Most of the inn guests' abilities were very well-suited to Cranmore."

Après-ski was a festive affair in the Elephant Room. "It was the place for skiers, no question about it," said Herbert. Jackets and ties were required attire in the dining room, but skiers could come directly from the slopes to the Elephant Room for après-ski, attired as they were on the slopes.

Carroll Reed's Eastern Slope Ski School instructors are shown celebrating New Year's Eve at the Eastern Slope Inn in December 1938. Shown from left are school chief instructor Benno Rybizka and fellow Austrian instructors Toni Matt, Otto Tschol and Franz Koessler. *Courtesy of North Conway Public Library.*

Tennis, Horse Shows and More

To further promote the inn, Gibson set out to provide guests with a stunning array of winter and summer sporting activities. In the summer of 1938, the inn and mountain inaugurated the Eastern Slope Horseshow, which brought nationally famous horses and riders from New York. Gibson also established the Golden Racquet Tourney, featuring the game's top tennis stars.

Babe Ruth—whose daughter Julia eventually married a local innkeeper of the Cranmore Mountain Lodge—also played in the inn's golf tourneys at the North Conway Country Club. (The North Conway Country Club now has several photographs on display at its clubhouse, showing the Babe in fine golf form.)

"I used to wait tables here when I was twenty, after I served in the marines for three years during World War II. That was back in the winter of '47. I waited on Hannes Schneider and his family—his son, Herbert, and

Skiers arrive at the Eastern Slope Inn after skiing nearby at Cranmore. The inn and Cranmore have long enjoyed a symbiotic relationship from the days when Harvey Dow Gibson bought it in the summer of 1937 through today. The inn since 1980 has been owned by Eastern Slope Inn Associates. *Courtesy of Dottie Crossley, New England Ski Museum.*

daughter, Herta. Henry Ford II, too—he'd dine after everyone else had left the dining room, but he'd make sure to tip everyone. I remember he'd ski at Cranmore, and when he left, he'd leave the new ski outfit he'd brought with him behind!"

The speaker at the time of the interview in 2008 was a bespectacled and still fit eighty-one-year-old retired builder from Massachusetts named Walter Hamil.

Hamil and his wife, Mary, were on a visit back to the inn when the impromptu conversation took place in the lobby. He said the dining room was located in a space that at the time was home to Eastern Mountain Sports and, since 2011, has been home to a used clothing boutique, It's My Girlfriend's.

Hamil said the dining room was able to accommodate 175 guests. "It was windows on both sides, with the north side overlooking the clay tennis courts in summer, which were turned into a skating rink in winter. We were paid ten dollars a week, and we'd get room and board, living in a dorm on the property—that office building over there now. Boys downstairs, girls upstairs. Every Friday night, the snow trains would roll into town, bringing a new bunch of snow bunnies north," said Hamil, noting that a ski pass at Cranmore cost employees just twenty-five dollars. "It was a great job," he said.

Mrs. Gibson Sells Inn and It Undergoes Transformations

Mrs. Gibson sold the inn in 1959 to a group headed by Charles Peter Pinkham, which ran it until 1971. Mrs. Gibson sold Cranmore in 1963 to Herbert Schneider and a group of investors who owned the mountain until 1984.

After a series of owners, the Eastern Slope Inn sadly closed its doors in 1976, the victim of the oil crisis of 1973 and mismanagement, according to former owner and general manager Pinkham in a 2008 interview.

The following year, Eastern Mountain Sports acquired the property and opened its sporting goods store on the ground floor of the inn and continued to operate the inn's restaurant.

The year 1980 saw a dramatic turn in the inn's fate: a limited partnership group, Eastern Slope Inn Associates, purchased the property from Eastern Mountain Sports, with the purpose of restoring the inn to its former glory. The restoration began with the inn's lobby and the second- and third-floor guest rooms. The walls were gutted, and new wiring, insulation, soundproofing, plumbing, fire-safety systems and a computer-controlled climate control system were installed.

On Friday, July 17, 1981, the Eastern Slope Inn resumed hotel operations fifty-five years to the day after its first opening. The following summer, the Eastern Slope Inn was officially listed on the National Register of Historic Places, owing to the role it had played in the economic development of the region's tourism and ski industry, as well as its architecture.

The inn's transformation into the modern era continued with the introduction of a vacation time-sharing program. Development continues today with the addition of cottages and other buildings adjacent to the main inn.

Every March, during the New England Ski Museum's annual Hannes Schneider Meister Cup at nearby Cranmore Mountain, the weekend's ski history lecture is held in the inn's Gibson Room, named after Mr. Gibson.

"I have to say," said Herbert Schneider in 2008, "Joe Berry has done a wonderful job bringing the inn back. It has always been the centerpiece of the village."

Just as Harvey Gibson and Harry Randall would have wanted.

CHAPTER 6
GEORGE MORTON'S SKIMOBILE

RECALLING NORTH CONWAY'S ONCE UNIQUE SKI LIFT

Gibson Gets His Lift

Once Cranmore developer Harvey Dow Gibson had acquired his mountain in January 1937 and the Eastern Slope Inn that summer, he next needed someone who could build him a new lift to transport skiers.

During Cranmore's first season of 1937–38, Gibson had rented a rope tow from Eastern Slope Ski School founder Carroll Reed. Reed moved it to Cranmore from Thorn Mountain in Jackson, where it had not operated during the first year of the ski school. Gibson also invited Reed to open a second branch of his ski school at Cranmore that season.

In his autobiography, published by his widow Helen Whitney Gibson in 1951 one year after his death, Gibson says he consulted with his friend W. Averell Harriman, developer of Sun Valley in Idaho, which had opened with the world's first chairlifts in 1936. They had been developed from an engineer recalling the design for banana-loading conveyor equipment used for tropical fruit ships' cargo, according to Jeff Leich of the New England Ski Museum in "From Pastime to Enterprise: Skiing Becomes a Business."

Gibson invited Harriman (then Union Pacific chairman, future diplomat during World War II and later the forty-eighth governor of New York) to North Conway to take a look at the area's potential, according to Gibson. "He was generous with advice in one respect in particular which proved to

Goodrich Falls mechanic George Morton had a reputation for being able to fix anything. Part of the team that created the overhead cable lift at Moody's Farm with Edwin Moody and Phil Robertson in 1935, he was hired by Cranmore developer Harvey D. Gibson in the spring of 1938 to come up with a new ski lift. The end result was the Skimobile, the lower part of which opened at Cranmore in December 1938. *Courtesy of North Conway Public Library.*

be invaluable," wrote Gibson in his autobiography's chapter on skiing. "He urged that we be sure to construct the best and most modern tramway in existence. He expressed the opinion that it did not make any difference what it proved necessary to charge to ride on the tramway, provided it was of a nature to appeal to skiers on which they could ride in comfort. He said that they would gladly pay the price."

Harriman recommended that Gibson find a "first-class engineer" and have him visit and study every tramway that had been built in recent years. He offered to have him visit Sun Valley to confer with his engineers, who could furnish him with blueprints. Gibson didn't have to look very far, however.

Gibson wrote in his autobiography:

> *In casting about as to the best engineer to engage for this purpose, and having had various experiences with a number of eminent gentlemen in their profession, I finally decided to obtain for the purpose a certain person who ran a garage about four miles from North Conway, while not a graduate of any engineering school, had demonstrated to me over a period of many years, that he often was the only person who could tell me what was the matter with my automobiles and fix them when such results had not been obtainable in Metropolitan centers. His name was George Morton.*

"Mechanical Genius"

Operator of a garage at Goodrich Falls that was still standing as of 2012 off Route 16 just north of Story Land, Morton had worked with farmer Edwin Moody and later Cranmore general manager and future Attitash developer Phil Robertson on building the lift at Moody's Farm in Jackson that later became known as the "Shovel Handle" once it was retrofitted in 1937 by Bill Whitney with shovel handles for skiers to hang onto, rather than ropes dangling from the overhead cable. Opened in 1935, it was the first such overhead cable lift in the valley and the second in the country, according to the New England Ski Museum's Leich in "The Ski History of Bartlett, New Hampshire."

Morton was a self-taught mechanical genius, according to his daughter, the late Marion Morton Randall (d. 2012). "He went through grammar school and later took a lot of correspondence courses," related Randall in a 2007 interview with the *Mountain Ear* at the base of Cranmore. "He was

Morton's garage in Goodrich Falls is shown with a Skimobile car out front. The cars were painted and stacked at the garage and then shipped to Cranmore, where they were assembled and put on line, according to Morton's late son, Parker, who worked on the lift side by side with his father. A total of sixty cars were hooked up for the first year of operation of the Lower Skimobile. *Courtesy of North Conway Public Library.*

always studying things engineering and electrical work, but he never went to college or anything. He grew up on a farm near Goodrich Falls, where he later had his garage. He was always just very handy," said Randall.

Gibson wrote that he paid a visit that winter of 1937–38 to Morton at his garage and told him what he would like to arrange.

The late Parker Morton (d. 1991), Morton's son, took the story from there in a summer 1988 interview with this writer. "Everyone knew of my father's reputation as a mechanic," said Parker, "and Gibson also knew that my father had put in a lift at Moody's Farm in 1935."

Although some accounts (including Gibson's autobiography) say that George Morton crisscrossed the country over the next two months after conferring with Gibson, looking at other designs, the sometimes cantankerous Parker said he doubted that. He said he "surely would have known," because he worked side by side with his father at the shop and lived with him at the time.

"As far as I know," Parker said in 1988, "Gibson came to my dad and said he wanted to put in a ski lift at Cranmore in connection with the hotel. He told my dad he could go anywhere he wanted, even California if necessary, to look at other lifts, but Dad, being the conservative Yankee that he was,

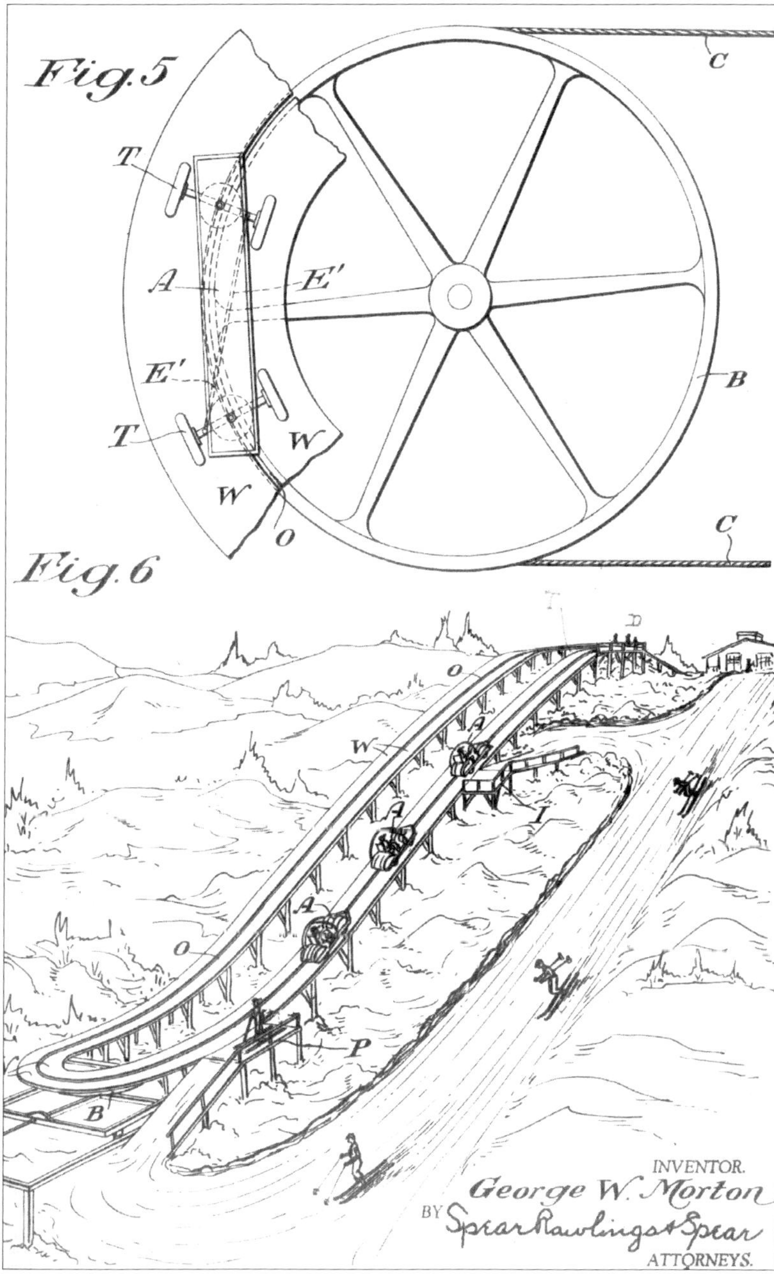

A photo showing one of the first drawings used by Morton in the application for a patent for the Skimobile. George Morton developed the overall plan, while his son Parker helped to draft it on paper, Parker said in a summer 1988 interview. A model of the Skimobile was shown at the New York World's Fair. The fair was chaired by Cranmore developer Harvey D. Gibson in 1939 and 1940. *Courtesy of North Conway Public Library.*

couldn't see the point of going away that far. He had his garage at Goodrich Falls to look after," Parker related, "so he couldn't afford to go all over the country. He knew there was a lift which had been installed down in Gilford in 1938, so he went there instead."

George Morton was not enamored of what he found in Gilford, where the country's second chairlift after Sun Valley's had opened at what is now Gunstock in the winter of 1937–38. According to Parker, his father especially didn't like the way his feet dangled from the seat of a chairlift high off the ground. When he returned home to Bartlett, he got to thinking about the cable cars in San Francisco he'd read about. Why not have a lift of cars on a track, attached to a cable that would pull them along?

When Parker returned home in the spring of '38, after graduating from the Wentworth Institute in Boston, his father had a job waiting for him. He needed someone to draft the engineering specs for a ski lift he was working on, and he believed that his son was the man for the job. "He told me his

George Morton's Lower Skimobile is shown during the second year of Cranmore's operation in 1938–39. The Lower Skimobile opened in December 1938. Carroll Reed's rope tow can be seen to the right of the Lower Skimobile. The rope tow was moved by Carroll Reed at Harvey D. Gibson's request from Jackson to Cranmore for the North Conway area's first lift-serviced season of 1937–38. *Courtesy of North Conway Public Library.*

idea and told me to draft it on paper. He had the big picture of what he wanted," Parker related, also always an inventive chip off the old block, "and I sketched it up for him. And that was that."

That summer, Parker created a small metal model of one of the proposed cars for the lift. Parker noted it was a "good thing" that he experimented with the model before moving onto the actual production cars. "Little problems arose which we wouldn't have known about, and which would've caused us some big problems later," he said.

During the design process, Marion Morton Randall remembered how her father used to have her practice sitting down at a dining room chair at their family's house, skis in hand. "He'd ask us to carry our skis, just to see how people might get on a lift," Marion related.

In 1988, Parker said, "Originally, the idea was to get on it while wearing skis, but then my father changed his mind because he figured the lift lines would be too long. So, he decided to make it so people carried their skis."

In his autobiography, Gibson wrote that he returned to Morton's garage two months later upon being informed that the inventor had come up with a plan for a lift. Morton invited Gibson upstairs to show him a model of what Gibson shortly thereafter coined the "Skimobile," according to Gibson's autobiography.

"After looking it over intently for some time," wrote Gibson, "I said to [him], 'You may be surprised, I might be just damfool enough to build one of those things.' So I proceeded to that objective, first applying for a patent for it, which eventually came through and which I later presented to the inventor."

1,800 Feet of Mechanical Wonder

Work crews began laying the track in July 1938. As construction got underway under the supervision of William G. Duprey, George and Parker kept working on the cars at the Goodrich Falls shop. With both men being mechanically inclined, father and son worked well in tandem, although Parker didn't recall there being too much said between the two as they tinkered.

"I can't say that Dad supervised me a bit, really, looking back. I'd get to a certain point, and I'd ask him, 'Is this what you meant?' Dad had the idea of what the end result should look like," Parker said, "but as far as the structure and design went, that was what I was there for."

Connie Davis Watson rides the Skimobile at Mount Cranmore. A frequent model, she was the first female president of the North Conway Chamber of Commerce and a devoted ski instructor in the Eastern Slope Ski Club Junior Program. *Courtesy of North Conway Library.*

The bullwheel for the lift arrived via coal car from the American Steel shop in Boston in July 1938. A 5,975-foot steel cable was attached to the bullwheel, and the cars were then attached to the cable. The bodies for the cars were made at a sheet metal plant in Gardner, Massachusetts, and then shipped to Morton's garage for painting ("Guess who did the painting?" Parker laughed), in patriotic shades of red, white and blue. (Sometime between then and later, a decision was made to paint all Skimobile cars red or green, their hues until its demise in 1990.) The cars were then crated and shipped to Mount Cranmore, where the lower section of the Skimobile trestle had been laid.

A total of sixty cars were hooked to the cable the first winter, with crews working in the cold fall rain to assemble them and get them on line. "We would have had more, but that was all we had been able to make that summer," Parker related.

Morton and son designed the lift's power station to be located at the midpoint, halfway up the mountain at the top of the Lower Skimobile.

"That's the best spot for it because it pulls the cars on the lower section," Parker said in 1988, when the lift was still operating, "which is far more efficient. It's easier to pull than to push something up a hill.

Getting the Kinks Out

Were there any problems when the lift got going on December 27, 1938? A few, but not many, according to Parker. In the beginning, the lift's cars featured pneumatic inflatable tires, which had to be inflated because they would deflate in the cold air. Those tires were later changed to hard rubber wheels, Parker said.

The biggest challenge that first winter proved to be the gearbox, which had really been built to run an elevator in a vertical position. "We had it horizontal, though, and we didn't have an oil pump, so the oil never got to it enough. We just kept shoveling snow on it all winter to keep it cool while it was doing all that work," he said.

Hailed as a revolutionary device that would change skiing forever, the lower Skimobile ran 1,800 feet up the side of Mount Cranmore and offered skiers convenience and, for that era anyway, speed. On New Year's Day 1939, it carried 1,065 passengers at a rate of about 255 per hour.

To the Top

While skiers everywhere hailed the Skimobile's development, an even bigger moment in the evolution of American skiing took place in February 1939 when it was announced that Cranmore owner Harvey Gibson had arranged to have internationally renowned skimeister Hannes Schneider released by the Nazis, who held the father of modern skiing as a political prisoner in Germany.

Upon his arrival in North Conway on February 11, 1939, Schneider took one look at Cranmore and immediately told Gibson that he had to expand to the summit. Work on the upper section of the Skimobile consequently began, extending the lift from the mid-station to the summit, a distance of two thousand feet, at a maximum grade of 38 percent.

When it was completed on August 1, 1939, Mrs. Harvey D. Gibson broke a bottle of champagne on a red Skimobile car at the halfway station to christen and officially open the completed tramway. More than two hundred passengers rode to the summit that first day, and the number increased thereafter.

At its full capacity, the Lower Skimobile had 150 cars, while the Upper Skimobile had 60, according to longtime lifts supervisor John "Hot Rod" Holmes. The Lower Skimobile had 3 boxcars and the Upper had 2, all equipped with plows in winter, Holmes said. They were used as freight cars to bring supplies up the mountain, according to Holmes—a man born the same month and year that the Lower Skimobile opened and a thirty-nine-year employee who took care of the Skimobile for twenty-two years.

To improve upon the old gearbox, which required so much snow to keep cool, a new gearbox was ordered from the Faulk Gear Company, and that made a big difference with the uphill efficiency and power of the lift. "That baby is 97 percent efficient, the best there is. They make 'em for steamboats. That solved the problem of having to throw snow on," Parker said in 1988.

SKIERS FLOCK TO CRANMORE

The lift continued to grow in popularity, attracting visitors in summer as well as in winter. Combined with Schneider's teaching and the growth North Conway experienced as a ski resort, the Skimobile definitely had made its place in history.

Rope tows had proliferated throughout the state before the introduction of the Skimobile, including in the Eastern Slope Region at places such as Oak Hill (late 1930s to early 1940s), Intervale Ski Slope (mid-1930s to early 1970s), North Conway Slope off the West Side at today's Birch Hill subdivision (1930s to early 1940s), Russell's Slope in Kearsarge (1930s to 1950s) and in Fryeburg, Maine, at Jockey Cap (1936–1938), according to New England Lost Ski Areas Project author Jeremy K. Davis. Together with a single chair and surface lifts at nearby Belknap Ski Area (now Gunstock) in 1937 and the state's opening of the Cannon Mountain aerial tram in summer 1938, however, Cranmore's Skimobile put skiing on a different level, according to Jeff Leich, executive director of the New England Ski Museum.

"Whether with a tram at Cannon, a chairlift at Belknap or the Skimobile at Cranmore, these areas had more pieces of the puzzle that are recognizable with what we today would call modern ski resorts," said Leich in the fall of 2012.

The Skimobile, as seen from Cranmore's deck in 1953. Cranmore's sunny exposure has always made it a favorite for sun worshippers—hence the popularity of the phrase "Tan More at Cranmore." *Photo by Dick Smith.*

A ceremony was held on December 27, 1939, exactly one year after the first Skimobile car made its way up the lower Skimobile. An inquiring reporter noted that while Harvey Gibson was there, George Morton wasn't. That intrepid reporter, in the company of an official from the Eastern Slope

Ski Club, finally located the mechanic and inventor in his element, working under a semi-wrecked automobile in the grease pit of his garage. He was still waiting for other ski resorts to place orders for his invention, orders he expected but that never came.

A second "skimobile" was built in 1959 at the Homestead Ski Resort in Hot Springs, Virginia, but Morton never got any royalties, since the lift featured enough of a change in design to make the Skimobile's patent non-applicable, according to his son.

"The Skimobile went counterclockwise; theirs went clockwise. Ah, patents—all they do is give your secrets away to your competitors," spat Parker in disgust in the 1988 interview, which took place at his home and machine shop on the Conway end of West Side Road. That house was later purchased by neighbors and razed after Parker's passing in 1991.

Keene Byrd, a historian for the Homestead at Hot Springs, said the lift was replaced by more popular chairlifts in 1970 at Virginia's first and oldest ski area. "It wasn't popular for very long. People didn't like having to carry their skis, especially when the newer chairlifts were coming along, so they replaced it," said Byrd in an October 2012 interview.

REBUILDING THE SKIMOBILE

The Lower Skimobile was rebuilt in the summer of 1945 and completed to the Halfway Station in the spring of 1946. Steel runners were put on the track, and Douglas firs were used to rebuild the Lower Skimobile. The project also included construction of a new base lodge. (That lodge was remodeled in 1986–87 and again in 2010.)

Other than the version at Homestead in Hot Springs, Virginia, Skimobiles never caught on elsewhere, due to the prevalent use of chairlifts at other resorts. Even Cranmore bowed to the new technology when it installed its East Chair on the backside of the mountain in 1955 (being replaced for the 2012–13 season with a new triple, to be named in honor of Herbert Schneider).

Rift Over Lift Proceeds

Problems arose between Gibson and Morton that were never resolved regarding payment for his services, according to Parker. The original agreement between the two, signed on October 31, 1939, granted Morton an annual license fee of 5 percent of the net profits of the Skimobile after operating expenses and taxes but not before special charge-offs or reserves had been deducted from gross receipts.

The license was to last five years, after which all rights to Skimobile patents would revert to Morton and he would be free to sell others anywhere except within fifty miles of North Conway.

Morton and Gibson never patched up their differences, although Morton did agree to Gibson's request that he take a look at a problem the lift experienced in 1948 or 1949—for a price, according to Parker. "I don't hold it against Gibson; I always blamed it on his lawyers," Parker said in 1988.

Gibson died on September 11, 1950, at age sixty-eight and George Morton on December 27, 1961, at age seventy, exactly twenty-three years to the day after the baptism of his invention. He invented other devices over the years, but none brought him as much renown as the Skimobile.

Herbert Schneider (left) and Parker Morton are shown in 1988 at the base of the Cranmore Skimobile invented by Morton's father, George Morton, in 1938. The lift was dismantled in the spring of 1990. *Photo by Tom Eastman.*

So Long to the Skimobile

The Skimobile's end came during the tenure of Ed Mank, who together with partners as Mount Cranmore Inc. purchased the mountain from Herbert Schneider and Babco partners in 1984.

Former general manager Marilyn Miller said in an August 2012 interview that she lost sleep over the decision to take out the much-beloved lift. "It was not an easy decision for any of us. Everyone loved the Skimobile and had an emotional connection to it," said Miller, still troubled over the decision. "But costs were going up; it cost a lot to maintain and for insurance. We could no longer justify the costs of operation, and its usefulness was no longer viable," said Miller, who left Cranmore in 1994.

Miller said several of the cars were donated to locations around the village. One stands at Connie Davis Watson Park off Main Street in North Conway Village; another is located at the New England Ski Museum in Franconia. A good number were purchased by a now deceased collector named Richard Veasey, said to be from the Haverhill, Massachusetts area.

In an October 2012 interview, Peter Pope of Intervale and Biddeford, Maine, said he purchased several Skimobile cars from Veasey in 2002. Pope says he then sold them to people who wanted to own a bit of Cranmore history. "Mr. Veasey bought them from Cranmore after it was decommissioned. I'm not sure how many he had or what happened to the others. He was not in good health at the time, and he wanted to make a deal. I'm unwilling to say how many I sold other than to just say a handful—anyone I had dealings with had to have a personal connection to Cranmore, because otherwise, it's just scrap, right?" said Pope, who grew up skiing at Cranmore.

That practice of selling old lift chairs was resumed in 2012 with a different decommissioned lift at Cranmore: this time, with the dismantling and replacement of the East Chair that had been in operation since 1955. It is being replaced with a new triple that will greatly change how the mountain is skied, notes general manager and president Ben Wilcox. The Skimobile, the East Chair, nearby Wildcat Mountain's old 1958-opened gondola cars… it seems there's no limit to how far enthusiasts will go to own a piece of local ski history.

New Uses for the Mountain

After the Skimobile was removed, Miller, the former general manager, said a halfpipe was put in the Skimobile's space to the north of the South Slope, allowing Cranmore to cater to the growing snowboarding market. In 2001–2, a terrain park was installed on the middle and lower part of the mountain within the Skimobile's corridor.

"If there was any way we could have kept it and had the terrain we needed it never would have come down…Maybe in hindsight, seeing how the mountain has evolved, we should have preserved a small part of it at the bottom," said Miller.

The wooden Skimobile trestle was recycled for the Cranmore Tennis Stadium bleachers. The stadium was used in the 1980s to host several concerts, including by the Beach Boys; Crosby, Stills and Nash; John Denver; the Fabulous Thunderbirds; Bonnie Raitt; Elvin Bishop; and Dwight Yoakam, to name a few.

The bleachers were later removed, the last tie to the Skimobile. The stadium courts were bulldozed in 2010, and that area is now the site of Cranmore's tubing park.

The Skimobile's name lives on, however, as the namesake for the high-speed fixed-grip detachable Skimobile Express quad chair that was installed by then owner Les Otten in 1995. It's less sentimentally beheld than the original but a lot quicker and much appreciated.

CHAPTER 7
HANNES SCHNEIDER
THE SKIMEISTER AND CRANMORE

By 1939, North Conway native son and world financier Harvey Dow Gibson's goal of transforming North Conway's economy was taking shape. He had acquired Cranmore Mountain in January 1937; bought the former Hotel Randall in the summer of 1937, renaming it the Eastern Slope Inn and announcing it would henceforth be open winters as well as summers; and commissioned the building of the Skimobile, the lower part of which opened in December 1938. He bought Carroll Reed's two ski schools in the summer of 1938.

Next, he set about his most ambitious plan: using his international financial clout to obtain the release from Nazi custody of Austrian ski great Hannes Schneider. Schneider had been arrested following the Austrian Anschluss of March 1938, when Hitler's Germany and Austria were united. Jailed, Hannes was eventually allowed to be held under house arrest in the home of Dr. Karl Roesen in Garmisch-Partikirchen, Germany. Roesen had been Hitler's court-appointed attorney in the "Beer Hall Putsch" trial of 1924 and had high connections to Hitler's command and German skiing, according to historian E. John B. Allen of the New England Ski Museum in "Schneider and the Germans."

While the rest of the world wondered how to get Hannes free, Gibson went to work. Going through an intermediary, the noted philanthropist

Hannes Schneider (in 1938) taught the world how to ski with speed and control through his crouched, progressive-turned Arlberg technique. Friend of royalty and the common man alike, Schneider (1890–1955) began teaching skiing at a ski school at the Hotel Post in St. Anton, Austria, in 1907. An outspoken anti-Nazi, he was arrested after Germany annexed Austria in the Anschluss of March 1938. Held under house arrest in Germany, his detainment caused an international uproar and eventually led to his coming to run the ski school at Mount Cranmore in February 1939. *Courtesy of Stefi Reed Hastings collection.*

Although then only fifteen years old, young Hannes (third from right) was already regarded as one of the leading ski innovators in Europe when this photo of Austrian ski instructors was taken in Zurs in 1906. *Courtesy of New England Ski Museum.*

and world financier made an offer for Hannes to come to North Conway and take over the ski school at Mount Cranmore. Hannes refused, still harboring dreams of someday being able to return to his beloved St. Anton. A subsequent, unauthorized trip home, however, convinced Hannes that the Austrian Nazis would never allow him to go back.

When the mayor of Garmisch thereafter asked Hannes to take over all four of the ski schools of that resort, Hannes consequently accepted, since Garmisch was located close to home. The Austrian Nazis were furious when they got word of the plan, however, and plotted to sneak into Garmisch at night and kidnap Hannes. Tipped off to the plan by the German Gestapo, Dr. Roesen had Hannes quietly sent away to Berlin. The Austrians arrived but had to leave empty-handed, after which Hannes retuned to Garmisch. He then sent word to Gibson's representative in London that he would, after all, like to accept the offer to come to North Conway.

Concurrently, Hitler was having trouble with Germany's financial affairs. The country lacked funds to pay interest on its war debt from World War I, and Hitler dispatched a personal emissary, Dr. Hjalmer Schacht, to London on behalf of the Reichsbank to get an extension of time. One of his first appointments was with Harvey Gibson's London representative. Gibson controlled a vast finance business that had loaned millions to the German government deposed by Hitler. That money was now due, and Schacht was told that Germany's economy might crash if it failed to maintain its credit rating. Unless, that is, the Nazis were somehow able to release a certain prisoner named Hannes Schneider and allow his family to leave the country with him.

A deal was struck, with Gestapo chief Heinrich Himmler personally signing all the necessary papers. No terms of the deal were to be reported, with the official explanation given that Hannes was "an old friend of Harvey Gibson's."

As a result, Gerard Fairlie and North Conway's Bill Clapp wrote in *Flight Without Wings*, some members of the American press insinuated that, since he never spoke out against the Nazis, Hannes must have been a follower of their policies. Nothing could have been further from the truth, according to Hannes's son, Herbert Schneider. "My mother went through hell when my father was under [house] arrest in Germany. My sister and I also received some rough treatment. Those were tough times," Herbert noted in 1988. "We were very grateful to be leaving the country."

America Greets the Skimeister

The negotiations took some time, but on January 9, 1939, Hannes was given his papers and told to meet his family in Munich and get out fast. Traveling to Paris by rail, the family—wife Ludwina and children Herbert and Herta—took the train to Cherbourg, where they boarded the *Queen Mary* and set sail for New York on February 4. Met by Gibson in New York on February 9, the family boarded a snow train on February 10 and arrived at North Conway's train station at 7:40 a.m. on February 11.

That morning marked a milestone in the history of North Conway. Led by Mr. and Mrs. Gibson, both of whom had traveled with the Schneiders on the overnight trip north from New York City, the Schneiders left the train and walked under an archway of ski poles in the park held by 150 schoolchildren enrolled in the Eastern Slope Ski Club Junior Program.

On hand to greet the great skimeister and family were four of his instructors who had preceded him to the Eastern Slope Region—Benno Rybizka, Toni Matt, Franz Koessler and Otto Tschol—along with eighteen of his American instructors from the Eastern Slope Ski School.

Hannes Schneider demonstrates his Arlberg technique to students in St. Anton. After serving as a ski instructor for the Austrian army during the First World War, he returned to the Hotel Post. In 1921, a film came out based on the Arlberg technique. He formed a semi-independent ski school where, by 1924, he had formalized his method of instruction. *Courtesy of Christof Thony, Klosterdal Museum.*

Hannes Schneider was invited to teach in Japan in March and April 1930. In addition to teaching hundreds of skiers at a time, the skimeister gave numerous lectures and was fêted at several receptions. To this day, Schneider is still revered in Japan, where three statues have been created in his honor. *Courtesy of New England Ski Museum.*

Among those who were there that morning was Norma Ashnault Haynes Wassall, later director of the children's ski school and a member of the class of 2012 Cranmore Snowsports Hall of Fame. Also there were Marion Morrell Owen and John Cannell. "In one of those pictures of the arrival, my brother Wally is right there with two ski poles sticking straight up. He went on to ski at Dartmouth," said Wassall, now eighty-three and the matriarch of a skiing family with long connections to Cranmore. "It was a big thing in the town when Hannes arrived. We kids thought he was stern, and we were afraid of him at first—but Hannes was good to kids, and he was wonderful to me. He could not have been nicer or more considerate."

Cannell remembers his mother waking him up to get to the station. "I was nine. She didn't want me to miss it," said Cannell.

Said Owen, sister of ski instructor and later Story Land founder Bob Morrell, on the seventieth anniversary of the Schneiders' arrival, "We were told about his coming in school. It was so exciting!"

First Run at Cranmore

With Benno Rybizka acting as interpreter, Hannes and his family that first day were escorted by Gibson to their new home on Grove Street in North Conway for breakfast. Gibson then took Hannes to the old West Side Slope (off what is now Birch Hill) for a morning ski session. There, he was greeted by his local instructors: Bob Beckley, Dave Stiles, Bob Emerson, J. Arthur Doucette, Francis Galorneau, Hugh Emerson, Francis Savard, Arthur Callan, Shirley Jodner and William Duprey.

After lunch, they were back skiing, this time at Mount Cranmore. Standing at the top of the South Slope, which in those days was cut only halfway up the mountain, Herbert Schneider remembered how his father told him, "Come on, Herbert. Let's show them how it's done." Halfway down the slope, they stopped. "Well, Herbert," Hannes said, "it's not St. Anton, but we're going to love it here." "And he was right," Herbert recalled in 1988. "We did!"

Tap Goodenough, winter sports editor at the time for the *Boston American-Record*, recalled watching the Schneiders make their way down the South Slope that first day. "Swooping like a snow bird down Cranmore Mountain, this expert was the cynosure of all eyes that memorable day as he gave a grand exhibition of down-hill running, using his renowned Arlberg technique. Although completely in control," Goodenough wrote, "his boards seemed to have wings as he traversed the slope in perfect Christiania turns with plenty of vorlage."

The first suggestion Hannes made to Gibson at the bottom of the slope was straightforward and direct, according to Herbert. "The South Slope was all that had been cleared at the time, and Father told Mr. Gibson that the trails had to be cleared to the summit," Herbert recalled. "Mr. Gibson just told Father, 'Hannes, I've gotten you here, and from now on this will all be your job. Now go put Mount Cranmore on the map,'" Herbert related.

On the Map, and Then Some

Hannes did that and much more. Skiing had been established in the Eastern Slope Region at such areas as Whitneys' Slope in Jackson and on local Civilian Conservation Corps–cut trails and other smaller slopes served by rope tows. Hannes's arrival, however, elevated North Conway's reputation as a ski resort to new heights. The opening of the lower Skimobile that year, combined with the mountain's proximity to rail service and Hannes's presence, made Cranmore the place to ski in the East.

"His very serious ski school policy, patterned after his first school in St. Anton, brought the famous people to Cranmore in its early days. The Fords skied there, as did the Rockefellers, Mellons, Rothschilds and Saltonstalls," noted the late Herman Ostermaier, one of Hannes's first ski instructors and the former owner with his wife, Trudy, of the Oxen Yoke Restaurant and Slalom Lounge of North Conway (today the offices of the Glen Group). In a letter to this writer in 1988 from his home in Colorado, Ostermaier added, "Through Carroll Reed, Dr. Harold Shedd, Benno Rybizka and Hannes Schneider, Cranmore became one of the first three important ski centers in northern New England. Hannes' first major work, to make slopes instead of trails, was a major step in this direction."

With Hannes at the helm of the ski school, the goals that Harvey Dow Gibson had envisioned when he acquired the mountain two years earlier were fulfilled. Skiers flocked to North Conway to ride the unique Skimobile, and Hannes brought fame to the resort, all of which benefited the economy of Gibson's old hometown of North Conway.

Sadly, Ludwina Schneider died from cancer six months after the family's arrival. Hannes and their children pressed on as best as they could, adapting to their new life.

Hannes and Gibson became fast friends and remained that way until Gibson's death in 1950. Hannes served as president of the ski school and a member of the Eastern Slope Ski Club's board of directors. He also actively oversaw the club's Junior Ski Program and races.

In addition to his skiing duties, Hannes designed and laid out the trail system at Cranmore, utilizing the mountain's topography and sunny exposure. He also experimented with soil erosion prevention techniques. The Kandahar, the Koessler, the Gibson, the Arlberg…all these trails were the results of Herr Schneider's imagination and expertise.

When not working on Cranmore's trail system in spring, summer and fall, Hannes worked as a ski area consultant and ski equipment advisor. When time allowed, he took to recreational pursuits with the same abandon he had brought to skiing. Always an avid hunter and fisherman, he continued those pursuits in America and also became an avid golfer. After being introduced in the winter of 1943–44 to frequent North Conway visitor Babe Ruth, Hannes also became an ardent baseball fan, rooting for the Yankees. The two sportsmen took an instant liking to each other, according to Herbert

Hannes Schneider was the world's first international ski film star. He teamed up with German filmmaker Dr. Arnold Fanck to make several ski films in the 1920s, culminating with *The Fox Chase Engadine*, which showed Schneider as the fox being chased by a group of "hounds" on skis. He and Fanck also produced a ski book, which was translated to English as *The Wonders of Skiing* in 1931. *Courtesy of Christof Thony, Klosterdal Museum.*

Hannes and Ludwina Schneider and children Herbert and Herta were enthusiastically welcomed when they arrived in North Conway via train from New York City on the morning of February 11, 1939. Riding the rails with the Schneiders was Harvey D. Gibson (right). On hand to greet them were Benno Rybizka (far left), director of the Eastern Slope Ski School, and 150 Eastern Slope Ski Club Junior Program schoolchildren, who formed an arch with their ski poles under which the Schneiders passed. *Courtesy of North Conway Public Library.*

Schneider, and understandably so: Hannes was to skiing in Europe what Ruth was to baseball in America.

Hannes was a familiar sight on Main Street during his sixteen years in North Conway. With an Austrian cape on his back, he'd make his way to the post office, which was then located in the Gibson Block, greeting townspeople along the way. "Hannes was as much a part of the North Conway scene as the mountain [Cranmore] itself," writer Pat Harty noted in a *Boston Globe* article following Hannes's death in April 1955. "He was never too busy to stop and say an encouraging word to some neophyte on the slopes. His ready smile and its hospitable warmth made every skier feel at home, in the north country town."

"Everyone was in awe of him, of who he was and what he had done," noted the late Kay Reed, whose husband, Carroll Reed, founded the Eastern Slope

Hannes Schneider (left) and Harvey D. Gibson are shown during a radio interview with Lowell Thomas that was aired in March 1939 from the Eastern Slope Inn, nearly a month after Gibson had obtained Schneider's release from Nazi custody and brought him to North Conway to direct the ski schools at Cranmore Mountain and Jackson. Gibson had purchased Carroll Reed's two ski schools in summer 1938 and then worked behind the scenes to bring Schneider, his wife, Ludwina, and their children, Herbert and Herta, to North Conway. Schneider's arrival helped to put Cranmore and the Eastern Slope Region at the forefront of skiing. *Courtesy of North Conway Public Library.*

Ski School as an American branch of the Hannes Schneider Ski School in Jackson in the winter of 1936–37. Added Carroll, who died in 1995, "He had a tremendous warmth about him. He was very Austrian, and strict, but he could put his arms around you and tell you what to do in a gentle way."

Roland O'Neal grew up in North Conway. Now retired and living in Sleepy Hollow, New York, he was the older brother of Damon O'Neal, a promising young racer who was killed at age sixteen in March 1959 in a downhill training run at Sugarloaf, USA, Maine. He shared the following story about Hannes in an interview in September 2012:

> *With Hannes, it was not so much "bend zee knees" as it was "follow the skis." In the early 1950s, I was part of a trio—Skip Hodgkins, Dave Lucy and I—who had coffee at Bill White's restaurant (where Horsefeathers now welcomes the*

> *hungry) after a movie on Main Street in North Conway and had the privilege on occasion to sit with Hannes and discuss skiing. He knew us all from our time in the elementary and high school ski programs with our Cranmore lessons. I'll never forget that time when he said, "I want to see you early tomorrow so you can learn to slalom on ice." Ice was the operative word in the early '50s on the North Slope at Cranmore during those winters when the mountain seemed to be snow-starved.*

O'Neal said Hannes went on to describe his youth in Austria when "there was little worry about our White Mountain ice, and he could maneuver in the Alps with his edgeless, two-grooved, seven-foot, six-inch downhill skis."

"He extolled the virtues of 'not pushing the turns too much.' His suggestion was just to 'gleede" (glide) through the gates," said O'Neal.

The young high school skiers got to Cranmore early the next day for their agreed-upon on-the-slopes meeting with the great skimeister, then in his sixties.

> *We met him at the top of the slope, at which time he promptly told us to go down to the bottom of the first pitch and observe his motions. I can still see his nearly ballet-like movements in great arching turns across what now seems like blue ice. After descending about half the slope, he stopped and raised his ski pole, motioning us to come down and emulate his motions. Of course, we could not, but he was understanding...He urged us to form a line behind him as he looked over his shoulder to monitor our techniques. When we got to the bottom, he had us follow him again up the Skimobile to the second platform in the woods. We got off and proceeded with our "lesson" to the base of Cranmore, where the ski school was forming...and where the paying customers were waiting for their "private" lessons. We had had ours...and enough wisdom, inspiration and technique to last a lifetime. We saw Hannes several times in the next two years before he passed away. We would ask us to join him for coffee at Bill White's, and he elaborated other movements for deep powder (sometimes in a gruff voice), but the conversation always ended with the dictum, "Follow the ski."*

A MAN OF INTEGRITY

Former Schneider instructor Otto Lang gave insights to Hannes's character in an interview in 1988.

Lang was twenty-two when he applied for an instructor's job in Schneider's ski school at St. Anton in 1930. Hannes had up to that time always utilized

Hannes Schneider (left) and Benno Rybizka are shown at Cranmore soon after Schneider's arrival in 1939. *Courtesy of North Conway Public Library.*

local boys from St. Anton in his ski school, but the Tyrol region at the time was seeing an increasing number of French and English clients, and Lang spoke both languages fluently. Consequently, Lang, a resident of Salzburg, was hired as the school's first "out-of-town" instructor.

When Lang first met him, Hannes had just returned from a tour of Japan, where he had taught thousands to ski, a trip that was heralded in newsreels

According to Herbert Schneider, people used to ask his father, "What else is there to do when there's snow on the ground but ski?" To which Hannes would respond, "Yes, what else is there to do when there's snow on the ground but ski?" Over the past few years, Cranmore Mountain Resort would answer that question by saying that in addition to skiing, visitors may now ride a Mountain Coaster or a Giant Swing, go snow tubing, ride the Soaring Eagle Ziprider and more. It's all about having fun outdoors. *Courtesy of North Conway Public Library.*

and news stories throughout the world. His ski school, which he had founded at the Hotel Post in St. Anton in 1907, was renowned as Europe's finest. His Arlberg technique, which began with the snowplow and progressed to the parallel turn, had become the way to ski throughout Europe.

His fame was spread worldwide with the release of two films made with Dr. Arnold Fanck, *Fox Chase in Engadine* (1921), and *The White Art* (1924), a technical film that later served as the basis of an instructional book published with Fanck, *The Wonder of Skiing*. The films captured the beauty of the mountains and the sport, showing Hannes hurtling down precipitous slopes in a display of skiing mastery that had never been seen before. Lang noted that he initially was awed by the prospect of working for the legendary skimeister.

"I had never met Schneider," Lang wrote in an October 1987 article in *SKI Magazine*, "but the first sight of him left an indelible image that has never changed. Schneider's head looked like a character study by an Austrian wood-carver. A shock of black hair partially covered his high forehead," continued Lang, who published his autobiography, *Bird of Passage*, in 1994. "His aquiline nose was prominent, as were his dark brown eyes, which gazed upon you with penetrating scrutiny but also displayed a mischievous twinkle."

Lang left St. Anton in 1935 to join fellow Austrian Sig Buchmayr (1907–1964) at America's first ski school at Peckett's on Sugar Hill in Franconia, New Hampshire, and stayed until the spring of 1936, when he traveled west to appear in a ski documentary on the Arlberg technique, filmed on Mount Rainier. Inspired by the conditions, Lang envisioned opening his own ski school there the next season as an American branch of Hannes's St. Anton school, the very same year that Carroll Reed opened the Eastern Slope Branch of the Hannes Schneider Ski School in Jackson, New Hampshire. "I asked Hannes if I could use his name for the school, and he said I could, at no cost. We became great friends, and it was more than just a business deal," Lang noted.

Later director of the Sun Valley Ski School and a film director, Lang attributed much of his success in life to his lifelong friendship with Hannes Schneider. "He was an inspiration to me always, and more than just a father figure to me," said Lang, who joined Herbert Schneider (1920–2012) at Cranmore's 1989 "Flight Without Wings" celebration, along with such fellow skiing luminaries as Aspen developer Friedl Pfeifer (1911–1995), two-time U.S. National Downhill Champion and legendary 1939 American Inferno winner Toni Matt (1920–1989), instructor Otto Tschol (1909–1995), Vail developer (and former Bartlett resident) Pete Seibert (1924–2002) and ski filmmaker Warren Miller, to name but a few. "He was a role model of how a man should be," said Lang.

PROUD TO BE AN AMERICAN

Beginning in 1947, Hannes never missed the opportunity to return to St. Anton every fall to hunt, particularly after his daughter, Herta, married a St. Anton native, Franz Fahrner. He never seriously considered moving back to Austria, however, noting that he was now an American and that things in the old country had changed. Some suspected he wanted to return to his homeland and take everything over again, but such a possibility was not in his mind. But when the name of the Hannes Schneider Ski School was changed to the Arlberg Ski School, Lang said it hurt him deeply.

Interviewed a year before his death by the *Christian Science Monitor*, Hannes said there really wasn't any contest. "If I were faced with the choice between going back and staying in America, I wouldn't need to think for a second. Why? Because," he said, "I like America and I am grateful to the Americans for the opportunities they gave me when I was down. In this country anybody can get anywhere if he works."

Ski racing champion, innovator of the Arlberg technique, instructor to millions the world over and friend to all on North Conway's Main Street, Hannes was truly mourned when a severe heart attack felled him on April 26, 1955. He had spent the previous day surveying the backside of Mount Cranmore, laying out the area's East Slope. He was upstairs in the home now occupied by his grandson, Christoph, on Grove Street in North Conway Village when the end came. Messages of sorrow were sent from all over the world, but perhaps the most poignant was penned by editor Paul K. Blanchard in the *North Conway Reporter*:

> *How wonderful that the late Harvey Dow Gibson provided us with Cranmore Mountain and made possible the coming of Hannes Schneider, who, down through the years, has shaped the trails and slopes in a symmetry of beauty which can be preserved to ever remind us of the meaning of Hannes' life. Skiing at Cranmore today, one cannot help but feel a kinship of spirit with Hannes, a man who accomplished much and overcame great odds, both in Europe and here in North Conway, and who truly loved life while creating winter fun for all. His legacy lives on every time a skier takes to Mt. Cranmore's slopes on a sunny day much like the one that first greeted Hannes on that February afternoon back in 1939.*

CHAPTER 8

HERBERT "ZIP" SCHNEIDER

A LIFE ON THE SLOPES

To understand why Herbert Schneider's nickname was "Zip," all you had to do was take a sweeping, graceful run with him down the Skimeister or Arlberg trails at his beloved Cranmore. Smooth, wide giant slalom turns were his style, executed seemingly effortlessly. .

In an interview in his original hometown of St. Anton am Arlberg, Austria, in April 2005, Herbert related that the nickname had been given to him in 1940 by Walter Maguire, who drove him and best friend Toni Matt to a ski instructor certification examination given by Roger Langley on the old Whiteface Trail in New York. He became known as "Zip," and the name stuck.

His other moniker, of course, was "Son of the Father of Modern Skiing," as Herbert was the only son of legendary ski instruction pioneer Hannes Schneider, inventor of the Arlberg Technique.

Just as he carved smooth tracks down Cranmore's sunny slopes, Herbert cut a respected niche of his own in the ski industry that was his life for seventy-three years. He received several awards over the years. In addition to being named to the U.S. Ski Hall of Fame in 1992, an honor his famous father received in 1958, he received the New England Ski Museum's Spirit of Skiing Award in 2009 and was made an honorary lifetime member of Professional Ski Instructors of America (PSIA) and of the Ski Club Arlberg of St. Anton, Austria, in 2010.

The father-and-son team of Hannes (left) and Herbert Schneider is seen at the base of Mount Cranmore. The two worked as a team, with Hannes directing the ski school until his death in 1955, after which Herbert assumed directorship. Herbert and partners purchased Cranmore from Mrs. Helen W. Gibson in 1963. They sold the area in 1984. During his years as general manager, Cranmore was known for its family-friendly children's programs and for Herbert's community spirit. *Schneider Family Files.*

General manager and part owner with Boston partners of Cranmore from 1963 to 1984, Herbert served as a consultant and as the area's skiing ambassador thereafter.

A Life on the Slopes

In a skiing slopeside interview in 1988, the sixty-eight-year-old, still smooth-skiing Herbert related what North Conway and Cranmore had meant to him and his family. Stopping on the Hurricane Trail, on the mountain he had by then called home for fifty years, Herbert related the allure that skiing held for him all his life and for his father before him. "People used to ask Father, 'What else is there to do when there's snow on the ground but ski?' And Father used to reply, 'Yes, what else is there to do when there's snow on the ground but ski?' That's the way it's been for me, too," Herbert observed with a cheerful smile.

A skier since the age of three, Herbert's lifelong skiing résumé included everything from instructing to being an examiner, ski instruction book author and general manager.

In his later years, he and son Christoph divided their time between North Conway and his original hometown of St. Anton, but there was never any question about which one was home. Like his father before him, he received numerous offers after the war to teach elsewhere, but he stayed at Mount Cranmore, partly because he considered North Conway his adopted hometown and also because he felt an obligation to serve the mountain.

"Father never forgot what Mr. and Mrs. Gibson had done for him and our family, and I felt the same way. My roots are here, and when I look at this mountain, I'm proud of the role Cranmore and our family played in the development of skiing," Herbert said.

Like Father, Like Son

Herbert said at the age of eighteen, he began teaching at Mount Cranmore under the direction of his father soon after their arrival in February 1939. "I couldn't speak any English back then, and I hadn't done any teaching in Austria. I'd go out with [future Story Land co-founder and early local

Sergeant Toni Matt (left) and Corporal Herbert Schneider at rest during training with the U.S. Army during World War II. Lifelong friends, Matt and Schneider hiked to the top of Tuckerman Ravine together when Matt won the legendary 1939 American Inferno. "I carried Toni's sandwich," laughed Herbert years later in telling the story of Matt's thrilling schuss of the Tuckerman Ravine headwall in that summit-to-base race, which Matt won with a time of six minutes, 29.2 seconds. *Courtesy of New England Ski Museum.*

American ski instructor] Bob Morrell and listen to what he told ski students, or I'd hang out with [fellow original local Eastern Slope Ski School instructors] Arthur Callan and Benno Rybizka," Herbert related.

Cutting the Trails

Following the Schneider family's arrival in 1939, Hannes Schneider took one look at Mount Cranmore and promptly told Gibson that new trails from the top of the mountain had to be cut if the area was to prosper. Gibson agreed, and work commenced. Work also began on the Upper Skimobile, which was completed in August 1939.

Herbert recalled memories of trail clearing in the old days. He spent his first summer in North Conway clearing brush and tossing rocks with his father.

Joining Herbert on the trail crew in 1939 was his lifelong friend and soon-to-become skiing legend, Toni Matt, who had come to North Conway just prior to the start of the 1938–39 season. "Toni and I split this ledge here, and we used only wedges and bolts. We cut the trails that summer using only handsaws and axes," Herbert marvelled. Was it hard work? "Oh, sure," he laughed, "but you bet it kept us strong. No question about it!"

Just two months after the Schneider family's arrival, Herbert accompanied Matt on the hike up Mount Washington for Matt's famous schuss of the Tuckerman Ravine headwall en route to his sensational victory in the American Inferno of April 1939. Herbert did not compete in that race, always joking that his job was to carry Matt's sandwich for him.

Herbert became a certified instructor in 1940 and also initiated his racing career. He placed second behind Matt in the first Gibson Trophy Cup Race held at Mount Cranmore that year, a prestigious race that was a big draw at Cranmore through 1966. His highest ranking occurred in the U.S. Nationals in Aspen, Colorado, in 1941 when he placed eleventh in the downhill, sixth in the slalom and eighth in combined.

Matt, as usual, raced to first overall in the championships that year. "Of course," Herbert laughed, "in all my years of competition, I was always overshadowed by Toni, including my days in St. Anton."

Bronze Star Bravery

When World War II broke out, North Conway's ski business prospered, with trainloads of skiers arriving to learn skiing and keeping Herbert and his fellow instructors busier than ever. Herbert became an American citizen in 1943, and, along with Matt, joined the army in August of that year.

Herbert Schneider (back row with wife Doris) is shown at 1989's "Flight Without Wings" celebration at Cranmore with members of the Morton family (left) and the Woodbury family (right), both of whom played key parts in Cranmore's history. George and son Parker Morton (seated left) created the Skimobile in 1938. Wendell Woodbury (seated right) was Cranmore developer Harvey D. Gibson's nephew. The celebration marked the fiftieth anniversary of the arrival of the Schneiders from Europe. *Photo by Sharon McNeill,* Mountain Ear.

Like many fellow Eastern Slope skiers, Herbert joined the Tenth Mountain Division Ski Troops and was stationed as a ski and rock climbing instructor in Camp Hale, Colorado. The division next was sent on training maneuvers in Texas before being shipped overseas to Italy. It was during a routine patrol near the Appenines there in 1945 that Herbert was awarded the Bronze Star Medal when his native tongue helped avert a disaster.

"Two of us had found a minefield," Herbert related, "and we were ordered to determine its size." Herbert went left, the other GI went right and that other GI—Bill Douglas—soon found himself attracting the attention of a few German sentries. To divert them away from his friend, Corporal Schneider craftily called out to the sentries in his native German, drawing the guards away from Douglas, who was able to escape and make it back to safety.

An American in St. Anton

The ultimate irony of Herbert's war years occurred in July 1945, when he paid an unauthorized visit to St. Anton at the end of the war after completing a mission with two other men to procure supplies in nearby Innsbruck. "Innsbruck was only sixty miles away from St. Anton, which I figured was close enough for me to go home for a visit," Herbert noted.

Reaching St. Anton, the GIs celebrated the birthday of Herbert's sister, Herta, at his father's former Schneider Sporthaus. This initially aroused some concern from the local residents, none of whom had recognized Herbert. "My aunt looked over and saw these American GIs celebrating, and not realizing that one of them was me, she thought to herself, 'Hmmph! Typical Americans, acting like they own the place,'" Herbert laughed.

A member of the U.S. Ski Hall of Fame and a lifetime member of the Professional Ski Instructors of America, Herbert Schneider was at home both in his native Austria and in America. He is shown in April 2005, standing before the house in Stuben, Austria, where his father, Hannes, was born in 1890. Young Hannes used to strap on his crude skis and bomb down the slope in front of the house, coming to a stop by intentionally barreling into bales of hay that were stored in a barn at the base of the slope. *Photo by Tom Eastman.*

Returning home after the war in 1946, Herbert resumed teaching at the Hannes Schneider Ski School. He also became involved as a director of the Eastern Slope Ski Club and served from 1947 to 1962. Following his father's death in April 1955, he took over as president of the ski school.

Herbert Schneider was one of the founders of the Professional Ski Instructors Association in 1961 and served on the board until 1972. Together with partners, he purchased the ski area from Mrs. Helen Gibson in 1963.

As president of the ski school and as general manager, he oversaw the expansion of the Eastern Slope Ski Club Junior Program at Cranmore. He once told an interviewer that he strongly supported that program because it gave an opportunity for every local schoolchild to learn how to ski.

"During my time as president of the ski school, we had over 500 children per year participating in the program. The ski school supervised the teaching of skiing while Mt. Cranmore provided the lifts free of charge," Herbert said, noting that the Junior Program had grown to provide instruction for nearly one thousand Mount Washington Valley youngsters a year. "I always let the kids ski for free to give them a chance to learn. We're a ski community in Mt. Washington Valley," he said, "and this is a sport which they can continue to enjoy all their lives."

In 1966, Herbert married former flight attendant Doris Beaudet of Hartford, Connecticut. They had two sons, Hannes and Christoph.

In 1967, Herbert authored the ski instruction book *Let's Go Skiing*. During his years as general manager, Cranmore hosted many ski events, as well as the Volvo International Tennis Tournament from 1975 to 1984 and the World Mud Bowl in 1979.

Although Herbert was the first to admit he was often frustrated by the unwillingness of his out-of-town fellow partners to invest in new improvements during his later years as general manager of the ski area, he was still proud of his family's role in the development of skiing and of Mount Cranmore's contributions to ski history. "There was never a question," he said in that 1988 interview, "that I would be involved in the ski business, when you consider the entire family background of my father's ski school and my mother's running of our ski and souvenir shops."

He and his partners sold Cranmore in 1984. He remained a consultant to the team of successive owners over the years and was esteemed as the area's ski ambassador.

Gentle-natured and of good humor in all his dealings, he annually presided over the New England Ski Museum's Hannes Schneider Meister Cup, as well as annual Tenth Mountain Division gatherings.

Herbert Schneider (second from left) congratulates Team Cranmore One on its victory over a second-place-finishing St. Anton team at the New England Ski Museum's 2000 Hannes Schneider Meister Cup. Shown from left are John Linne, Ed Bradley, former valley Olympian and ex-pro skier Tyler Palmer and Stefan Karnopp, grandson of Carroll and Kay Reed. The Schneider Meister Cup is held at Cranmore every March. Mountain Ear *photo by Tom Eastman.*

He received several awards over the years. In addition to being named to the U.S. Ski Hall of Fame in 1992, he received the New England Ski Museum's Spirit of Skiing Award in 2009 and was made an honorary lifetime member of PSIA and of the Ski Club Arlberg of St. Anton, Austria, in 2010.

A True Valley Treasure

Outpourings of respect and gratitude were expressed by many in the ski resort community of Mount Washington Valley upon learning of Herbert's death in June 2012 at age ninety-two.

Ski Hall of Fame inductee Tyler Palmer perhaps summed up Herbert's contributions best. Palmer, who was named to the Hall of Fame with fellow valley resident Phil Gravink of Jackson as part of the class of 2012, said:

Racer John Hughes (left) and Herbert Schneider are shown at the Hannes Schneider Meister Cup at Cranmore in the early 2000s. Herbert skied until the age of eighty-six, often racing with is fellow Tenth Mountain Division veterans from World War II. Mountain Ear *photo by Steve Eastman.*

> *How do I put this? He was kind of like the "Godfather of Skiing" as far as I was concerned. When I was a kid, we skied every day at Cranmore. My mother would pick us up at John Fuller School and we'd run like the devil to get on the Skimobile and up Cranmore to get some runs in before it got dark. Herbert would let us ski for free. He created a great life for my brother and me in skiing. I got to appreciate him a lot more when I got to go to Europe and St. Anton to race—he was my connection to that world from the start. He was so calm and placid. He had a very good perspective on the valley and the sport. I absolutely appreciate everything he did for me, the sport and the town—he covered it all.*

Ben Wilcox, general manager and president of Cranmore Mountain Resort, agreed that they don't make any nicer guys in the ski business than Herbert Schneider: "He was so kind and supportive to me in my eight years here at Cranmore as general manager. I drove him down to new owner Brian Fairbank's house on Lake Winnipesaukee, and I remember how on our way down and back how sharp he was, not only for ski history but also about the ski business. He had such humility, of how to treat people, and I was always so impressed by his kindness."

Steve Rice of CNL Financial Group worked with Herbert during 1989's "Flight Without Wings" celebration under the Mank ownership days and, later in his role with CNL, helped to finance the Fairbank and O'Donnell purchase. "A warm and gentle man, Herbert was loved and respected by those fortunate enough to know him or work with him. As general manager, he led Cranmore through important growth years and taught generations of skiers about the sport he loved. Herbert," said Rice, "exuded pure joy for carving turns under any conditions, and he remained an active skier until late in life. He will be missed by all of us who will attend Cranmore's seventy-fifth this winter, whether in person or in spirit!"

CHAPTER 9

EASTERN SLOPE SKI CLUB

CREATING LOCAL SKIERS (AND A FEW OLYMPIANS)

Mount Cranmore has been home to many races over the past seventy-five years, both professional and amateur, drawing some of the greatest names in American skiing to its sunny slopes. Perhaps the most famous of the races of old were the Gibson Trophy Cup Races, initiated in 1940 by Mr. and Mrs. Harvey Dow Gibson and continued until 1966 (there was no snow in 1964 and, consequently, no race, but that's another story). Proceeds of the race always benefited the Eastern Slope Ski Club Junior Program.

The Gibsons conceived the race as an annual open giant slalom primarily to stimulate racing interest within the Eastern Slope Ski Club, which presented the race, as well as to attract many of the top racers in the East to Cranmore. The Gibsons offered a trophy for the men's division, another for the women's field and a first, second and third prize for each division.

During its heyday from the late 1940s to the late 1950s, the Gibson Race attracted some of the best international racers, with only ten Americans

Opposite, top: Paula Kann (Valar), named to the 1948 U.S. Olympic Team, and ski racing sensation Toni Matt were the wunderkinds of racing at Cranmore in the 1940s. Both natives of Austria, Kann won the women's title in the Gibson Trophy Cup Race six times from 1942 to 1947, retiring the trophy twice, while Matt—winner of the legendary 1939 American Inferno on Mount Washington and U.S. Downhill Champion in 1939 and 1941—won the Gibson Cup four consecutive years before World War II and once afterward before moving west to Sun Valley. *Courtesy of New England Ski Museum.*

Race day at Cranmore in March 1951. Skiers line up at the top of the North Slope for their run. This photo was to be part of a *Life* magazine spread by photographer Martin Bovey Jr., but the piece never ran. *Courtesy of Stefi Reed Hastings.*

winning the laurel during the entire history of its running. Toni Matt, Paula Kann, Edi Mall, Anne Johnson-Jones—they all share the distinction of being the only skiers to retire the Gibson Trophy Cup by winning the race at least three times.

Both natives of Austria, Kann and Matt won the race every time they entered, with Kann winning the women's division an incredible six consecutive times from 1942 to 1947 to retire the trophy twice. The legendary Matt—winner of the 1939 American Inferno on Mount Washington, and a 1939 and 1941 U.S. downhill champion—won the first Gibson Race in 1940 and virtually owned it through 1943, after which he became an American citizen and entered the service for war duty. After the war, he won the Gibson in 1947 but missed his chance to retire a second trophy when he moved west to Sun Valley and never entered another Gibson Race.

Two-time winners of the race include Waterville Valley developer and two-time Olympian Tom Corcoran, who won it in 1957 and '59, as did fellow Olympic team member Penny Pitou. Also winning two trophies were Mary Stowell (1961 and '63) and Norton Webber Jr. (1962 and '65). Other winners of the Gibson Race included such famous skiers as Edgar Bering Jr., who took Matt's place on the winner's stand and became the first American to win it in 1944; 1952 Olympic great Othmar Schneider of Austria; and Chiharu "Chiki" Igaya of Japan.

Tyler Palmer—2012 U.S. Ski Hall of Fame inductee and a product of the Eastern Slope Ski Club Junior Ski Program who went on to compete in the 1972 Winter Olympics in Sapporo, Japan, along with his brother, Terry, and fellow Mount Washington Valley resident David Currier—raced in the last Gibson Race ever held in 1966 when he was fifteen. He notes it was far from memorable, laughing that he fell at about the fourth or fifth gate. "My brother, Terry, foreran the course, and he was good. But at that time, I wasn't. I was really small in those days, the smallest kid in my class," Palmer noted.

The future World Cup and professional racer recalls he was excited to be invited to compete in the last Gibson, noting he could barely go to sleep the night before.

> *I was just barely a Junior B racer, and that was the first chance I had to race against the "big boys." I remember getting up at 5:00 a.m. the day of the race and heading to the mountain to walk the course, which was held on the Arlberg that year. And the thing I remember the most is being so excited, yet looking up to see John Clough, one of the hot shot college racers, looking over the course beside me and yawning. That blew my mind.*

Mount Cranmore and all of Mount Washington Valley have a proud ski racing tradition, with several local skiers having progressed to the U.S. Ski Team and Olympic level. Shown here at a June 2011 fundraiser for the Damon O'Neal Scholarship at Cranmore were (from left) promising racer Ace Tarberry of Conway, 2010 Olympian and current U.S. Ski Team member Leanne Smith of Conway and 1972 Olympian Tyler Palmer of Kearsarge. *Photo by Stefi Reed Hastings.*

Added his younger brother, Terry, "I foreran the course when I was a seventh grader that year, and I would have finished in the top five, had I been racing. For me, that was a day I remember because it told me I was competitive, even with the best in the East as a young Junior III, which was an inspiration to dream of becoming an Olympian."

The race was renewed in 1977 and again for Cranmore's fiftieth-anniversary "Flight Without Wings" celebration as a fun alumni gathering. The Sise Cup Masters Race Series now annually holds the

Conway-raised 2010 Olympian Leanne Smith rose up from the Eastern Slope Ski Club Junior Ski Program at Cranmore to excel as a racer for Kennett High (pictured here), the University of New Hampshire and the Mount Washington Valley Ski Team before being named to the U.S. Ski Team. The daughter of Joe and Paula Smith, she is the sister of Kennett High ski coach Laurel Zengilowski. *Photo by Lloyd Jones,* Conway Daily Sun.

Gibson Masters Race, according to the Eastern Slope Ski Club's 1936–2006 anniversary booklet.

The valley has been home to several other Olympians over the years, including Kann (1948), Imogene Opton (later Fish) ('52), Brooks Dodge ('52 and '56), Gilford's Penny Pitou (1956 and '60), Abbi Fisher ('76 and '80) and cross-country ski racers Carl Swenson ('94, '02 and '06) and Marcus Nash ('94 and '98). Cross-Country Ski Team Olympians from other areas but who are now living in Mount Washington Valley are Maine Ski Hall of Famer Jack Lufkin, now director of sales at the Grand Summit Hotel in Bartlett and second director of the Jackson Ski Touring Foundation in 1973; and Sue (Long) Wemyss, now of Great Glen Trails Outdoor Center, who competed in the 1984 Sarajevo Olympics after graduating from Middlebury College in Vermont. Lufkin competed out of Rumford, Maine, at the 1968 Grenoble Olympics.

Leanne Smith, Olympian

Joining the local Olympic ranks in 2010 was Leanne Smith, twenty-five, of Conway. A member of the 2012 U.S. Ski Team who is looking forward to the 2014 Winter Olympics, Smith shared her thoughts in the fall of 2012 about what Cranmore has meant to her development as a ski racer, starting out with the Eastern Slope Ski Club Junior Program when she was a grade schooler at Conway Elementary School.

> *I am very thankful that I was able to grow up at Cranmore. Over the past few years, I have been fortunate enough to travel to a lot of different resorts, small ski areas like our own and beyond. I've noticed how much character Cranmore has and, most importantly, people who are very passionate for the sport. Skiing as a youngster has so much to do with your love and enthusiasm for the sport as you get older. The passion for it has to grow inside you. The Rattlesnake program, the Junior Ski Program and being on the Cranmore Race Team instilled those in me. I had the opportunity to ski all the time and to be with great teachers who shared their knowledge with me. I would not be where I am today without their ability to inspire and educate me as a young girl.*

She praised the efforts of Tyler Palmer, as well as those of Dave Gregory of the Mount Washington Valley Ski Team, an organization that was named the top ski alpine club in the country in 2012 by the U.S. Ski and Snowboard Association (USSA):

> *Any athlete who has worked with Tyler Palmer only has good things to say. Not only Tyler but also the entire group of coaches at Cranmore during my childhood was amazing. They taught me to enjoy skiing and they taught me to ski with confidence, which in turn made me want to ski even more. Tyler was a superstar in my eyes, so naturally I wanted to listen to everything he had to say. And as I've gotten older I've realized how much he revolutionized the sport in his day and how he grew to be one of the best coaches out there. I appreciate any time I get to spend with him; he is one of a kind.*

She was equally laudatory about the late Herbert Schneider. "Everyone who has spent time at Cranmore knows that Herbert Schneider is a legend," said Smith. "His family's story is incredible in itself, and they brought their passion to Cranmore and they're responsible for how Cranmore has grown over the years."

EASTERN SLOPE SKI CLUB JUNIOR PROGRAM

The development of local youth skiing, let alone of racing, is linked to the founding of the Eastern Slope Ski Club in December 1935 and the creation of its Junior Program in 1938. The program was founded by Chester A. "Chuck" Emerson (1889–1971). Emerson moved to Intervale to operate the Maple Villa (now the site of the Lodge at the New England Inn) during the Depression. He started the program to make sure that every child in the area who wanted to ski had the equipment to do so. Father of four sons, he watched them all grow into top skiers and helped others do the same.

Originally held at Cranmore, the program over the years has expanded to include Attitash, Black and King Pine, as well as cross-country at Bear Notch Ski Touring and Snowshoe Center, Jackson Ski Touring and Mount Washington Valley Ski Touring and Snowshoe Center, which includes Whitaker Woods.

As of 2012, the program served 1,098 students (932 alpine, 114 snowboard and 52 Nordic) in grades one through six from the following schools: Bartlett Elementary, Jackson Elementary, Madison Elementary, Tamworth Brett School, Freedom Elementary, the Waldorf School; and, in Conway, John Fuller Elementary, Conway Elementary and Pine Tree. New for 2012–13 was the Robert Frost Charter School.

The program is staffed by 350 to 375 volunteers, according to Bob Tagliaferri and ESSC Junior Program Committee board of directors chair Karen Dolan, who is a past Junior Program coordinator (a post now held by her daughter, Jes Dolan) and who serves as director of the Cranmore Snowsports School. "Just as Herbert Schneider always said, this program is unique because it lets every kid learn to ski, whether they can afford it or not," said Dolan in the fall of 2012.

The ESSC depends on member dues, as well as grants from such organizations as the Connie Davis Watson Foundation, the Red Parka Pub Challenge Cup held at Attitash every March and proceeds from the Used Ski and Equipment Sale, held at the North Conway Community Center every November since 1970. That tradition was founded by former coordinator and longtime youth skiing supporter Connie Briggs.

A father of two boys who have or are using the Junior Program, Tagliaferri sees it as a keystone for local kids that works through the cooperation of local schools, ski areas, touring centers, parents and volunteers (not all of whom ski, by the way—there's plenty of need for base lodge and parking lot help). "We're a skiing valley," said Tagliaferri, a former Black Mountain marketing director and Saco Bound owner who first began coming to the region as a boy from Cranston, Rhode Island. "The Junior Program is part of your heritage here."

Smith agreed, giving credit once again to the support that Herbert Schneider gave to young skiers through the Junior Program—some of whom (like her) grew up to be Olympians. "ESSC was the best thing that happened to the valley because of the opportunity that it gives every kid in the school district. Herbert built an environment at Cranmore where everyone could appreciate skiing, ski racing and the lifestyle that comes along with it. He was a great man, and his legacy will live on here in the valley within all that he created."

Helping children learn how to ski and ride is what it's all about for the Eastern Slope Ski Club Junior Program and for Cranmore's Arlberg Children's Center programs. The center (shown in background) features two surface lifts and a double chair, as well as a separate gentle slope where children can learn at their own pace. *Photo by Bill Lee, Cranmore Mountain Resort.*

CHILDREN'S SKI PROGRAMS

Just as the ESSC Junior Program helps local kids learn how to ski, all Cranmore skiers may enroll in the Cranmore Snowsports School's KidsRule Mountain Camps and other children's programs, all based out of the Arlberg Children's Center.

For those who want to race, the Cranmore Race Team (CRT) offers programs for racers ages eight to eighteen. A freestyle program is also offered. The CRT works with the Mount Washington Valley Ski Team (MWVST) for ages fourteen and fifteen and those ages sixteen and older, notes MWVST coach Dave Gregory.

It's all part of a local tradition of getting youngsters of all ages and abilities out on the slopes to enjoy a lifetime of fun.

CHAPTER 10
THE RACE FOR ALL TIME

CRANMORE RACING LEGEND AND INSTRUCTOR TONI MATT MAKES HISTORY

Cranmore skiers call legendary and late Austrian ski sensation Toni Matt one of their own, and with good reason. Matt emigrated from St. Anton to come to teach at Cranmore for the 1938–39 season. He was part of the wave of early Austrian instructors that included Benno Rybizka, Franz Koessler and Otto Tschol at Carroll Reed's ski schools in North Conway and Jackson. They were joined in February 1939 by Hannes Schneider and family after the skimeister's release from Nazi custody.

The boyhood best friend of Herbert Schneider, Matt was accompanied by Herbert on his hike up Mount Washington in April 1939 to compete in the third American Inferno. "I carried Toni's sandwich for him," Herbert laughingly recalled in a 2009 interview at Cranmore. "I had a very important role," he joked.

Held from the windblown summit, the race continued over the steep eight-hundred-foot Tuckerman Ravine headwall and down the twisting and narrow, tree-lined Sherburne Ski Trail to the base in Pinkham Notch. Up until 1939, the headwall in Tuckerman Ravine had generally been handled in a series of "check" turns. Matt, however, traveling at speeds approaching eighty-five miles per hour, took the headwall in a single long arc, leaving the nearly three thousand spectators assembled in the ravine literally awestruck. "They tell me there were thousands of people there that day," recalled Matt in 1989, "but I never saw or heard anyone on my way down. I was too focused on racing."

People are still talking about that 1939 Inferno seventy-four years later.

THE AMERICAN INFERNOS

The 1939 Inferno was the third summit-to-base race held on Mount Washington, with Hollis Phillips of the Appalachian Mountain Club winning the first in April 1933 with a time of just under fourteen minutes and American ski great Dick Durrance (1914–2004) winning the second inferno in April 1934 with a time of twelve minutes, thirty-five seconds.

A shortened race was held in 1935 from the summit to the floor of the ravine, but lack of snow kept it from running down to Pinkham Notch, so it was not termed an Inferno, according to Jeff Leich of the New England Ski Museum in his book, *Over the Headwall: The Ski History of Tuckerman Ravine.*

Matt was then just back from the championships at Mount Hood when he joined the field of forty-two racers who registered for the Inferno that spring, which was finally held on April 16, following two postponements. Unlike those two earlier attempts, Sunday, April 16 was nearly ideal, with bright skies, cold temperatures and high winds at the racers' backs on the summit and corn snow below. The conditions were an essential factor in aiding Matt in halving Durrance's previous record. The other factor was simply Matt's incredible performance.

After arcing down the headwall on his seven-foot, six-inch wooden skis, Matt later said he had intended to make two turns, but the snow had felt so good, he simply pointed his boards downhill and went for it. "I wasn't very familiar with the terrain, as I had never skied the headwall. I thought I had already gone over the lip and that I was halfway down. Instead, I wasn't even at the top yet," Matt recalled in a summer 1988 interview, often joking in his talks about the race with his thick Austrian accent and good humor that "you're lucky when you're 19, stupid and have strong legs" and that he "couldn't turn."

Matt said he nearly lost control and came close to hitting a tree near the base of the narrow Sherburne Trail in Pinkham Notch but held on for the victory. "The Sherburne Trail was very narrow. Maybe only 25 feet wide at most, and it was all grooved out, which could get you in trouble. The toughest part, though, was the transition on the floor of the ravine, because

Early Cranmore ski instructor and skiing legend Toni Matt was nineteen when he skied into history by making a downhill schuss down the steep drop of the Tuckerman Ravine headwall on Mount Washington in the 1939 American Inferno. The 1939 and 1941 U.S. Downhill champion, Matt had intended to make several turns on the headwall but started his schuss earlier than planned—most likely after the turn pictured here, notes the New England Ski Museum's Jeff Leich. *Photo by Adrian Bouchard, New England Ski Museum.*

there was no such thing as course preparation in those days. It was like a plowed field," Matt said, describing his never-equaled feat down the eight-mile run with some places approaching sixty-five-degree drops.

A Tuckerman Legend and Cranmore Racing Champion

Matt went on to win a second national downhill championship in 1941. He won the prestigious Gibson Trophy Cup Race at Cranmore from 1940 to 1943. He and Herbert Schneider served with the U.S. Army's Tenth Mountain Division Ski Troops during World War II. After the war, he won his fifth Gibson in 1947 and then moved west to teach at Sun Valley.

Matt suffered a severely broken leg in 1952 at Sun Valley, which ended his racing career. The leg was in a cast for three years before a surgeon operated successfully, thanks to the efforts of Lowell Thomas, famed broadcaster, ski promoter and frequent Eastern Slope skier. Matt then resumed skiing, teaching and coaching until his retirement from the sport in 1980 after serving as an official at the 1980 Winter Olympics in Lake Placid. He was inducted into the U.S. Ski Hall of Fame in 1967. From 1955 until his death in May 1989, Matt was the superintendent of the Quaker Hill Country Club in Pawling, New York—a job Thomas was instrumental in getting for him.

His performance in that legendary Inferno of April 1939 ranks as one of the most daring ski racing performances ever, even if he downplayed it himself. "I'm not trying to minimize it," Matt said prior to returning to Cranmore for the 1989 "Flight Without Wings" fiftieth-anniversary celebration, where he was greeted as a hero, "but everyone thinks I must have felt a terrific thrill or something. But all I was worrying about was to stand up and get out to the bottom of the headwall and then over the little headwall to the Sherburne Trail. I certainly wasn't thinking, 'Oh, what a thrill it is to schuss Tuckerman Ravine.' It was a mistake I made, really, in that I schussed further up than I had planned to, that's all."

Toni Matt (center), winner of the 1939 American Inferno on Mount Washington and a four-time Gibson Trophy Cup Race winner at Cranmore, is shown at Cranmore's 1989 "Flight Without Wings" celebration with 1984 Tuckerman Giant Slalom winner Eric Pendleton (left) of Jackson, New Hampshire, and 1972 Olympian Tyler Palmer of Kearsarge, New Hampshire. Palmer was runner-up to Franconia's Duncan Cullman in the shortened, so-called Bobtail Inferno, held in Tuckerman Ravine in 1969. *Photo by Tom Eastman,* Mountain Ear.

A Year of Reconnecting

Slowed down by a series of heart attacks in his sixties, Matt gathered with friends at Cranmore's "Flight Without Wings" celebration in February 1989. Among them were Herbert Schneider, Eastern Slope Ski School instructor Otto Tschol, Aspen developer Friedl Pfeifer and film producer and early Hannes Schneider disciple Otto Lang.

Earlier that year, Matt had made his first visit back to St. Anton. His son, Richard, recalled that his father had been worried how he might be received, since he and Herbert had fought for the Allies as American citizens. Instead, he was greeted warmly, with townspeople asking, according to Richard, "Toni, where have you been all these years?"

At the celebration at Cranmore, Matt posed for photographs with many fans, including 1969 Tuckerman Ravine Bobtail Inferno second-place finisher and 1972 Olympian Tyler Palmer of Keasarge and 1984 Tuckerman Giant Slalom winner Eric Pendleton of Jackson. He was in his element, back home at Cranmore.

Encouraged by his longtime friends, Matt took a run during the eight-day celebration at Cranmore for the first time in eight years. Steve Rice—then marketing director at Cranmore and now of CNL Lifestyle Properties Inc. of Florida—got to ski with Matt and Schneider, a thrill for any ski history enthusiast. Both then nearly sixty-nine, Matt and Schneider skied flawlessly, making classic big GS turns, according to Rice (see the foreword).

Back to the Ravine

A last treat awaited local Tuckerman ski fans on the fiftieth anniversary of his schuss, as Matt made his first trip back to the ravine in a half century on April 15, 1989. Accompanied by Richard and my brother, late *Mountain Ear* publisher Steve Eastman (1949–2008), who was there to take photos of the occasion, Matt was driven to the Hermit Lake shelter at the base of the lower headwall by longtime U.S. Forest Service snow ranger Brad Ray. Wearing a white Cranmore fiftieth-anniversary cap, the ski racing legend posed for photographs for Steve in front of the USFS Hermit Lake shelter below the lower headwall.

As for Ray, I remember his reaction when I had placed a call earlier in the week to see whether he might be interested in driving Toni Matt—yes, *that* Toni Matt—up to the ravine in the Thiokol, one day short of the fiftieth anniversary of Matt's legendary headwall schuss. "Boy, *would* I? I'd love to. I've told that story to so many people so many times, every time I go to the ravine, but I've never met him! So, yes!" exclaimed the usually reserved veteran snow ranger, who in 2000 went on to co-found with Al Risch of Madison the nonprofit Friends of Tuckerman Ravine organization, which is dedicated to preserving the backcountry ski experiences in the ravine and assisting the snow rangers with projects.

Matt was scheduled to give a talk that night at the Appalachian Mountain Club's Pinkham Notch Visitor Center, but there were so many people that the talk was moved just slightly north and across Route 16 to the Wildcat Mountain base lodge. "You know," he said, with a surprising and touching tear in his eye, "I've gotten a lot of mileage out of that race over the years. But seeing you people tonight really is something."

A month later, Richard Matt called this reporter once again, but this time with the sad news that he had found his father on the greens of the golf course in Pawling, dead of an apparent heart attack.

Friends of Tuckerman Ravine's "Tuckerman Inferno" Pentathlon

The memory of Matt's schuss has been kept alive every spring since 2001 with the Friends of Tuckerman Ravine's Inferno Pentathlon, held in mid-April and ending with a hike and ski run in the ravine, usually down Left Gully.

As longtime competitor and five-time solo Tuckerman champion David Lamb of Jackson has often said, he and fellow competitors feel a connection with Matt, Durrance and all those who came before. "Knowing what they did, on those old wooden skis, is really amazing. You can almost feel their presence when you're hiking up here for the ski run," said Lamb.

Racers in the 1952 Bobtail Inferno schussed the headwall from a standing start, but no one has ever done it from the summit as Toni Matt did when he vaulted into history in the April 1939 Inferno, the "Race for All Time."

—With Ann Bennett and Jeff Leich

CHAPTER 11

THE "CRANMORE FACTOR"

FROM LOCAL YOKELS TO THE FRIENDLY PENGUIN

Cranmore is the sum of all the dedicated people who have loved it over the years, whether as founders, skiers and riders or employees.

Foremost was the example set by the late Jimmy Mersereau. An employee of Cranmore since 1969, Jimmy made the mountain his home away from home. When he died suddenly in December 2009 at age sixty-six, the local skiing community was deeply saddened. From dressing up as C-more the Penguin (not many people knew that) to using his mechanical common sense to fix whatever problems he encountered, he was the glue that kept Cranmore together, according to general manager and president Ben Wilcox. "Jimmy was terrific. He cared so much for this mountain. We all loved him," said Wilcox. "Jimmy was responsible for many aspects of resort operations. He was a legend in the ski industry and a leader in environmental practices."

He was named an Olympic snow groomer for the 2002 Salt Lake Winter Olympics. He then led Cranmore's efforts to transform its snow-grooming fleet to use biodiesel fuels and helped design trails and glades at Cranmore.

Following his death, a memorable nighttime tribute was held in his honor in a parade of snow groomers and torchlight skiers down the North Slope.

Cranmore has played host to visits by several dignitaries over the years. Former First Lady and then-presidential candidate Hillary Rodham Clinton held a citizens' forum on health insurance at Cranmore in October 2007 while campaigning for the 2008 Democratic presidential nomination against eventual winner Barack Obama. She was welcomed by Cranmore general manager Ben Wilcox (left) and Cranmore operations director and biodiesel fuel pioneer Jimmy Mersereau. *Courtesy of Cranmore Mountain Resort.*

He posthumously received a U.S. Environmental Protection Agency Lifetime Achievement Award on the fortieth anniversary of Earth Day in April 2010. One year after his passing, "Jimmy's Run"—a trail he designed and built—was dedicated at Cranmore in December 2010. An approximately seven-ton granite slab was erected with a heartfelt bronze plaque mounted to it near the end of the trail. The memorial honors his forty years of dedication and love of Cranmore. A scholarship was created in his honor at Kennett High School for students pursuing environmental and/or wildlife sustainability.

His son, Johnny Mersereau, carries on his father's work as Cranmore's snow surfaces manager—yet another example of how generations of Cranmore skiers and employees remain committed to the area.

Locals on the Slopes

Weekly citizen racing has been a tradition at Cranmore since 1972. That was the year when Steve Sherlock and Herbert Schneider launched Local Yokel. Now known as Mountain Meisters, the ten-week Wednesday race series draws racers of all ability levels to Cranmore's North Slope racecourse.

"It's a social thing for most. But don't get me wrong—we in the race shack call Wednesdays 'World Cup Wednesdays' because for some skiers, it really is a serious, competitive thing," said staffer Eric Styffe, who works the shack with Ian Meserve, Doug McDonald, Danbo Doucet, Ed Bradley, David Fall and Dave Clancy, to name a few.

Eric Styffe (left) is shown executing some freestyle moves with a fellow hot dogger at Cranmore in 1973. Styffe, sixty-six, is a veteran of the Cranmore Snowsports School with forty-three years of experience heading into the 2012–13 season. He loves Cranmore's ski history and its place as one of skiing's pioneering areas. *Photo by Drew Phillips.*

SAFETY ON THE SLOPES

Drew Phillips, a forty-plus-year, still active Cranmore ski patrol veteran, has photographed many of the good and sad times at Cranmore over the years. Every trail brings memories, whether it's the Koessler, named after late Austrian ski instructor Franz Koessler; the Schneider; the Gibson; or even the Bandit, named after veteran ski patroller John MacDougall's wandering beagle, which used to leave his Kearsarge home to hop onboard the Skimobile for rides all day long.

Of his decades on patrol, Phillips says he has loved the camaraderie of working with people who loved what they did, all in good humor but with a commitment to safety on the slopes. "The patrol has always been a great bunch. We were kids when we were starting out working with dads, guys like [Bob] Dogger Haynes, Earl Cosby, Glenn Gray (my father-in-law)," said

The Cranmore Ski Patrol of 1989 during Cranmore's "Flight Without Wings" celebration, honoring the fiftieth anniversary of the arrival of Hannes Schneider and family. The ski patrol and the Cranmore Snowsports School staff have always been committed to Cranmore and its role in the ski community. *Photo by Drew Phillips.*

Started as the Local Yokel in 1972, Cranmore Mountain Meisters is said to be the oldest weekly recreational ski racing program in the United States. The ten-week season draws racers of all ability levels to the racecourse on the North Slope on Wednesdays. Competition is intense for some, while just seeing friends and making a few turns drives others. Above all, Meisters is about the sense of community camaraderie. *Photo by Brooks Dodge III.*

Phillips, noting that the new patrol director is Mike Malkin, a member of a local rock band when he's not patrolling. He'll be leading the new patrollers in the always unfolding Cranmore story.

The "Cranmore Factor"—It's All About People

Others who have shared a strong connection to Cranmore over the years include the Haynes family (led by matriarch Norma Haynes Wassall), the McDonalds and the Gilmores, which includes the Dolan branch of the clan led by longtime Snowsports School director Karen Dolan and her daughters, Jen and Jes.

"I knew I was going to be a ski instructor here when I was in junior high," said Dolan, who is also administrator of Mountain Meisters in addition to her Snowsports School job. She returned to Cranmore after ski racing in

Veterans of the U.S. Army's Tenth Mountain Division Ski Troops have long held their annual reunions at Cranmore over the years, largely due to Herbert Schneider, who won the Bronze Star Medal for bravery while on maneuvers in Italy in World War II. The reactivated Tenth is stationed at Fort Drum, New York, and annually sends over a contingent to ski in the New England Ski Museum's Hannes Schneider Meister Cup every March at Cranmore. *Photo by Drew Phillips.*

college in Colorado. "I remember following Herbert around in high school, telling myself that someday I was going to run a ski area. I know now that wouldn't necessarily be a good thing," she laughed, "but I knew that the ski industry was a good place for me to be. I love going out and teaching people and getting them over the hump. You make all kinds of friends, and it's rewarding for me to see all these kids who got to teach as their first job, and they come back in their thirties to say hi. We're actually planning a ski school reunion this March [as part of the seventy-fifth events]."

Tenth Mountain Division and Mount Cranmore

Due to Herbert Schneider's war service with the Tenth Mountain Division "Ski Troops" of World War II fame, Cranmore has long been home to nearly annual reunions of the legendary veterans, many of whom helped build North America's ski industry after the war. Aging veterans and active members of the Tenth often participate in the New England Ski Museum's annual Hannes Schneider Meister Cup Race.

The Ski Troops, as the men of the Tenth Mountain Division came to be known, were formed by the U.S. Army in the 1940s as a fighting unit on skis. Since 2001, the division and its four combat brigades have seen over twenty deployments to both Iraq and Afghanistan in support of Operation Iraqi Freedom and Operation Enduring Freedom, respectively, according to ski historian and author Jeff Leich.

C-more the Penguin is Cranmore's roving goodwill ambassador. He can most frequently be found helping youngsters roast s'mores at Schneider Square on Saturdays and special holiday Cranapaloozas, spreading the good cheer. *Photo by Bill Lee, Cranmore Mountain Resort.*

Snowsports Instructors Hall of Fame

Longtime Snowsports adult programs coordinator Don Newton serves as head of the Cranmore Snowsports Hall of Fame. Formed to honor those individuals who have made a significant impact on Cranmore snowsports instruction, the program inducts new members annually. Named in 2011 were Hannes Schneider, Herbert Schneider, Tenth Mountain Division veteran John McDonald, Danny Grant and Edi Mall. Inductees in 2012 were early Austrian instructor Benno Rybizka, Otto Tschol, Norma Haynes Wassall and Eric Styffe. A sign showing the names of the inductees hangs in Zip's Pub, named after Herbert Schneider.

C-more the Penguin

Personifying Cranmore's friendly spirit and warmth is C-more the Penguin. Loved by many, C-more greets visitors in Schneider Square and toasts marshmallows during events such as Cranapalooza. Children participating in the Cranmore Snowsports Children's Program at the Arlberg Children's Center enjoy seeing C-more around the slopes and receiving penguin stickers at the end of their lessons.

Community Connections

These Cranmore skiers and employees are but a sampling of a link to Cranmore's proud past and promising future, with Wassall, now eighty-three, being among the children who were on hand to greet Hannes Schneider and family in Schouler Park on their arrival in February 1939.

"It's right in North Conway's backyard, so there's a natural connection between Cranmore and the village," said former general manager Marilyn Miller in October 2012. "I often stop and think, 'What would North Conway have been like without Harvey Gibson, Carroll Reed and Hannes and Herbert Schneider?'"

Current general manager and president Ben Wilcox echoed Miller's thoughts in talking about how lucky he feels as a longtime local resident to now be serving the community and Cranmore. "I had gone to high school here, so I knew what Cranmore's role was in the community, but it wasn't until I started working here that I understood the full depth and regard that employees and the public have for this mountain, its history and its cultural strength," said Wilcox in a September 2012 interview. Starting out at Attitash after college and then Bretton Woods, he came to Cranmore in July 2004 during the Booth Creek era, replacing Ted Austin as general manager after he left to accept a post out west. He then helped to usher in the Fairbank-O'Donnell era in June 2010, staying on as general manager and president.

"There's a pride here that stems back to the Gibson, Hannes and Herbert Schneider days," Wilcox reflected. "The Fairbanks and Joe O'Donnell share that, and so does our staff. We're excited that our guests will be able to continue to count on Cranmore for generations to come."

CHAPTER 12

CRANMORE—VISION, INNOVATION AND PARTNERSHIPS

FROM SNOW GROOMING AND BIODIESEL PIONEERS TO YEAR-ROUND MOUNTAIN ADVENTURE

Starting in 1937 with Harvey D. Gibson, Carroll Reed and Skimobile inventor George Morton, Cranmore has been a pioneer in mountain recreation and ski industry innovation in the United States. First mountain manager Phil Robertson, who served from the installation of the Lower Skimobile from 1938 to 1963, led Cranmore in snow-grooming techniques as early as 1940—a necessity due to its westerly exposure.

After World War II, Cranmore continued to thrive, but it faced new competition from larger resorts that were being developed out west, several of them developed by many of Herbert Schneider's fellow U.S. Army Tenth Mountain Division veterans.

In December 1955, the East Bowl area was opened at Cranmore, having been laid out by Hannes Schneider with Herbert in the days before Hannes's death from a heart attack in April 1955. It was serviced by a new Roebling Double Chair. Among those on hand to help dedicate the lift was famed broadcaster and skiing proponent Lowell Thomas (1892–1981), long an ardent supporter of the Eastern Slope Region. Hired in 1938, Robertson left in 1963 to develop Attitash, which opened in 1965.

Mrs. Helen Gibson sold Cranmore to Herbert Schneider and Boston businessmen Harry and Sam Babain and fellow Babco partners in 1963. Cranmore added two new Mueller double chairs in 1963 and 1969.

Cranmore was an early innovator in snow grooming. Former mountain manager Phil Robertson—later of Attitash—began experimenting with snow-grooming tools as early as 1940, according to Jeff Leich of the New England Ski Museum. Cranmore installed snow making in the early 1970s with the aid of community business leaders. *Courtesy of North Conway Public Library.*

Cranmore installed rudimentary snow making in the early 1970s, aided by a group of North Conway business leaders led by Peter Pinkham, then of the Eastern Slope Inn.

Cranmore under Herbert Schneider's supervision was renowned for its strong support for the Eastern Slope Ski Club Junior Program, which helped to spawn a few Olympians. It was also known for its strong children's ski programs under ski school director Norma Haynes Wassall and for other programs, such as launching the Local Yokel recreational ski series with Steve Sherlock in 1972 (later renamed Mountain Meisters). Cranmore under Herbert also hosted pro races in the 1980s and served as the site of the Volvo International Tennis Tournament from 1975 to 1984.

MANK GROUP BUYS CRANMORE

Herbert Schneider and his four Babco partners sold the area in 1984 to a group led by real estate operator Ed Mank of Boston. After the sale, Herbert Schneider stayed on as a ski ambassador and keeper of his family's skiing legacy. Mank's team oversaw the development of seventy-four condominiums at the mountain (all of which promptly sold), the installation of the Lookout Triple Summit Chair in 1986 and 1987, the reconstruction and enlargement of the base lodge, the building of a second base lodge (now the Arlberg) and improvements to snow making and trails. The South Double Chair was opened in 1987–88.

After Rick Lavoie stepped down as general manager, local resident Marilyn Miller was promoted by Mank from a food service and management hiring consultant role to general manager in 1985. Backed by longtime employees Kevin Donovan, Arthur Carboneau, John "Hot Rod" Holmes and the late Jimmy Mersereau, Miller used their expertise in running the resort's on-mountain infrastructure.

Late veteran snow-making and mountain operations director Jimmy Mersereau (left) is shown in 1989 with then general manager Marilyn Miller and former facilities manager Kevin Donovan during Cranmore's "Flight Without Wings" celebration. Mersereau was a beloved fixture at Cranmore, making it his home away from home for forty years. Mersereau died at age sixty-six in December 2009. A trail that he built was dedicated in his honor a year after his death, named "Jimmy's Run." *Photo by Tom Eastman.*

"I think Ed hired me as general manager because he saw how I went to bat when the Doppelmayr lift was installed and although it ran, it wasn't operating satisfactorily and we had our 1986–87 season coming up and that was going to be our big new thing. I let them know in no uncertain terms that it had to be fixed, and I think Ed liked that. He approached me after that to ask if I would consider being general manager. That's when Jimmy [Mersereau] and I became very good friends, along with Kevin, because although I wasn't a [ski business person], they did know the facilities part, and we made a good team," Miller related.

Mank's group was lauded for upgrading Cranmore's infrastructure and for spearheading 1989's "Flight Without Wings" gala celebration on the fiftieth anniversary of the Schneider family's arrival. That eight-day event drew back to Cranmore such pioneering skiing luminaries as Herbert's sister, Herta Schneider Fahrner, of St. Anton am Arlberg, Austria, as well as Otto Lang, Friedl Pfeifer, Toni Matt, Paula Kann Valar, Vail developer and former Bartlett childhood resident Pete Seibert, Otto Tschol, ski filmmaker Warren Miller and several of Herbert Schneider's fellow Tenth Mountain Division World War II Ski Troops veterans, to name but a few. A highlight of the celebration was the unveiling of a statue at Cranmore's base of Hannes Schneider, created by Maine sculptor Ed Materson.

Miller said:

> *Steve Rice* [then marketing director and now with CNL Lifestyle Properties, the group that financed Cranmore's most recent sale in June 2010] *and I went to Ed* [Mank] *and laid it on the table what we wanted to do for the fiftieth, and he said go to it. We wanted to salute the legacy of Hannes and Herbert Schneider and all that this mountain meant to the community. He listened and let us run with it, even though we told him it would cost likely hundreds of thousands of dollars (which it did!). And one thing I have to say about Ed—other than a brief public acknowledgement that I intentionally gave him at the gala dinner, he didn't want any of the attention for what he did. That was just the way he was. He was not an easy person to get to know, and we had a lot of go-rounds, but I developed a tremendous respect for him in the years we worked together.*

Rice also praised Mank for his contributions. "I think Ed Mank deserves a lot of credit for investing in Cranmore's future," said Rice in the summer of 2012. "He kept a low profile, but his contributions to Cranmore were

Cranmore made headlines in 2003 when it became the first ski area east of the Mississippi to run its grooming equipment and other diesel vehicles on biodiesel (B20). The resort uses more than twenty thousand gallons of 20 percent biodiesel fuel each year, which results in a four-thousand-gallon reduction of conventional fossil fuel diesel. *Courtesy of Cranmore Mountain Resort.*

critical in keeping it in the game at the time and making the investment that has positioned it for what has taken place since."

A downside during Mank's tenure was a series of snow-challenged winters, which led to increased snow-making and operating costs. During Mank's ownership, another public relations challenge was management's decision to dismantle the Skimobile in 1990 due to rising maintenance and insurance costs (see chapter six).

Further changes occurred in the early 1990s. Interviewed in October 2012 from his Massachusetts home, Mank said that he and Bay Bank of Boston entered into a three-year management contract in 1991 to market the improvements that had been made. That contract expired following the 1994 season. Bay Bank subsequently hired Sno-Engineering of Littleton, New Hampshire, to manage operations while the bank sought a buyer.

Miller left after nine years in 1994, with local hotelier Ken Lydecker hired in her place as interim manager. He served from October 1994 until June 1995. "We had a lot of fun that year," said Lydecker, now co-owner of the Riverside Bed and Breakfast in Intervale. Despite having tight financial

In 2012–13, Cranmore Mountain Resort installed 60 new high-efficiency snow guns to offer more terrain and better snow surfaces. The snow guns represent a $250,000 investment—just part of the $8.3 million put into the resort since coming under new ownership in 2010. The purchase brings Cranmore's total of the high-efficiency snow guns to 378, serving 163 acres and sixteen miles of terrain. That number is up over 350 percent since 2008. *Photo by Bill Lee, Cranmore Mountain Resort.*

restrictions, Lydecker said, Cranmore retained its role as a community partner during his tenure, even helping to provide skis for the downtown holiday streetlight decorations in the village.

OTTEN BUYS CRANMORE

Les Otten of Sunday River, Sugarbush and Attitash bought the area in 1995. Otten's company (LBO Enterprises) brought in Tim Harris of Vermont as general manager. Harris and Otten's New Hampshire president, Phil Gravink of Attitash and Cranmore, oversaw the installation of a high-speed Doppelmayr detachable quad to the summit—the Skimobile Express, a benefit that Cranmore skiers are enjoying to this day.

"Les said the first thing we needed to do was get a quad in. We did that lift and shortened the old double for the racing program, as the unloading area up the mountain interfered with where we wanted to put the quad through. It really was the coming into the modern era for Cranmore," said Gravink in October 2012.

A 2012 inductee to the U.S. Ski Hall of Fame and a resident of Jackson, Gravink is an industry veteran who worked at Loon and Cannon and then was president at Attitash. He was then chief at both Attitash and Cranmore for Otten.

"Instead of bringing 800 to the top per hour like the old double on a busy day, the new quad increased it to 2,400 plus riders per hour," said Gravink.

DEPARTMENT OF JUSTICE ORDERS DIVESTITURE

To the chagrin of the community, Otten's ownership tenure at Cranmore was short-lived. In 1996, the ambitious ski mogul merged his LBO Resort Enterprises with S-K-I Ltd., forming the American Skiing Company, adding Haystack, Killington, Mount Snow, Sugarloaf and Waterville Valley. Later that year, however, due to anti-trust Department of Justice concerns, Otten was forced to divest of Waterville and Cranmore, while Pico was purchased.

He went on to success as part of the Boston Red Sox ownership team that won the World Series in 2004. He later sold his interest and is now involved in the Maine wood pellet energy business.

Shown at the press conference in June 2010 held to announce the sale of Cranmore Mountain Resort were general manager Ben Wilcox (second from left), new owners Tyler (left) and Brian Fairbank and Tom Lithgow of CNL Lifestyle Properties Inc., the group that financed the sale. *Photo by Jamie Gemmiti,* Conway Daily Sun.

Booth Creek Arrives

As part of the Department of Justice action, American Skiing sold Cranmore and Waterville Valley to George Gillette of Booth Creek Holdings in November 1996. Cranmore eventually was one of Booth Creek's nine resorts located in the West, Northwest and East. Snow-making improvements and new trails were built, along with a terrain park and tubing park.

Booth Creek's Ted Austin served as general manager from 1996 to 2004, fostering Cranmore's community role.

Biodiesel Innovation

During the Austin/Booth Creek era, Austin nominated longtime Cranmore staffer Jimmy Mersereau to be one of the groomers selected to work the 2002 Salt Lake Winter Olympics—an honor that pleased the much-beloved, dedicated Cranmore "Mr. Fix-It" dearly. In 2003,

Mersereau led Cranmore in becoming the first ski area in the East to use biodiesel in snow-grooming equipment.

A forty-year Cranmore veteran employee, Mersereau died in 2009 at age sixty-six, saddening the Cranmore community. A trail was named in his honor in 2010: "Jimmy's Run." (For more on Mersereau's contributions, see chapter eleven.)

THE WILCOX ERA

In 2012–13, Cranmore offers skiing, adventure rides and year-round family recreation for active-minded people. The resort's new owners since June 2010 have invested more than $8.3 million in improvements to Cranmore's snow making, lifts and year-round attractions at its Mountain Adventure Park. *Photo by Bill Lee, Cranmore Mountain Resort.*

After Austin left in 2004 to accept a position out west, Ben Wilcox, formerly of Attitash and Bretton Woods and a well-known, longtime resident of North Conway, was hired as Cranmore's general manager. Wilcox has continued to build on Cranmore's role in the community, bringing such events as Arts Jubilee to Cranmore beginning in the summer of 2007 and continuing the Jen's Friends Cancer Climb, held every September since 1998.

Under Wilcox, Cranmore has continued to celebrate its historic role in skiing, hosting the New England Ski Museum's annual Hannes Schneider Meister Cup every March. Mountain Meisters continues to be the largest recreational ski racing program in the country. He has also led Cranmore's welcome to freestyle and snowboarders with family-friendly terrain parks and bringing year-round activities to Cranmore.

Wilcox has assembled a dedicated team, with Kathy Bennett as marketing director; Rick Oaks as mountain manager; Glenn Harmon as director of operations; Beth Hamlin as human resources director; Becca Deschenes as assistant to the general manager; Kristen Barbin as Cranmore fitness director; Karen Dolan as Snowsports director; and Doug Holmes as finance director.

Always personally close to Herbert Schneider, Wilcox fostered Herbert's role as the mountain's esteemed skimeister until Schneider's death in June 2012 at age ninety-two. "I learned so much from Herbert and always enjoyed our talks," said Wilcox, who also fondly saluted the late Mersereau as the "guy who stuck it out through the years and who always gave Cranmore his best."

"Jimmy and Karen [Dolan] in particular have been part of the heart and soul of this mountain. They represent the team of people we have that shows such a commitment to this mountain and what it stands for," said Wilcox in the fall of 2012.

Fairbank Team Leads Cranmore

As noted earlier, Cranmore was sold by Booth Creek in June 2010 to the father-and-son team of Brian and Tyler Fairbank of Jiminy Peak and partner Joseph O'Donnell, owner of Bromley Ski Area. CNL Lifestyle Properties Inc., a Florida-based real estate investment trust, provided capital for the acquisition and improvements.

The area is undergoing a rebirth under the new ownership, with more than $8.3 million in investments as of 2012. Cranmore has expanded its winter tubing park and created an Indoor Adventure Center, while upgrading the Family Fitness Center. It has added summertime and year-round attractions, including a mountain coaster, mountain Segway tours, a Giant Swing, summer tubing, an aerial adventure course and a Soaring Eagle zipline. Every fall, working with Death Becomes You Productions, Cranmore offers a Ghoullog Halloween season attraction at both its base and summit.

For new capital improvements as of this writing, the old East Chair is being replaced for the 2012–13 season with a new triple fixed grip chair that was purchased from Wachusett Mountain in Massachusetts and retrofitted for Cranmore. To be named the Schneider Triple in honor of the late Herbert Schneider, it will run on the southwest side between the Koessler and Schneider Trails, starting near the juncture of Tommy's Trail and Beginner's Luck and ending on the summit.

Led by Wilcox and the new ownership team, all those who share a love for Cranmore are the new heroes in the Cranmore story as the resort enters its seventy-fifth anniversary season.

CHAPTER 13

A TOWN AND ITS MOUNTAIN

NORTH CONWAY'S FOUR-SEASON RESORT REVITALIZED

North Conway Village and Cranmore, its hometown ski area and now four-season resort, have had a symbiotic relationship for the past seventy-five years, each an integral part of the success of the other. That was the vision of original developer Harvey Dow Gibson, and it continues to this day under the new ownership team of father Brian and son Tyler Fairbank and partner Joe O'Donnell, who acquired the mountain in 2010 with financial backing from CNL Lifestyle Properties Inc.

General manager and president Ben Wilcox has been at the helm for nine years, hired by previous owners Booth Creek Resorts in 1994 after Ted Austin left. A Kennett High and University of New Hampshire graduate who worked at Attitash and then Bretton Woods, Wilcox appreciates Cranmore's role in American ski history and the mountain's relationship to the town.

Luckily for the town, he was in more than just a management position to move Cranmore's position forward. "Three years before Booth Creek left, they sat me down and said, 'We have to find a way to move our focus to the west, so we are starting to try and sell off our eastern partners.' They told me they'd like me to be in the forefront of that effort," said Wilcox in a summer 2012 interview.

With the help of former Cranmore marketing director and now CNL Financial Group senior vice-president and managing director Steve Rice,

Mount Cranmore and North Conway Village, as seen from the Conway Scenic Railroad's North Conway Train Station—the same view seen by Hannes Schneider and family as they disembarked on the morning of February 11, 1939. The town and the mountain have enjoyed a close connection since Harvey Dow Gibson first opened the area with lift-serviced skiing in January 1938. *Photo by Brooks Dodge III.*

Wilcox and Booth Creek found a viable partner who shared Wilcox's vision for the future and a respect for Cranmore's past: the Fairbank and O'Donnell team of Jiminy Peak of Massachusetts. "What moved Cranmore into a new era was the understanding that we were a diamond in the rough—we just needed a big hug," said Wilcox. "That hug was the Fairbank team."

Cranmore opened northern New England's first Mountain Coaster in 2010. The Mountain Coaster is part of Cranmore's year-round attractions. *Photo by Bill Lee, Cranmore Mountain Resort.*

The first meeting he had with the Fairbanks also included Rice, Wilcox said. "We had a good meeting, talking of the opportunities that Cranmore had for the future to evolve into a year-round business and its role with the community. The exciting thing about Brian and Tyler is they understood Cranmore's history and the special role it had and the possibilities it had."

As Wilcox spoke, the father-and-son Fairbank team nodded in agreement and also praised the role that Rice had played from the outset as someone who relished the mountain's vaunted past with the Schneiders while having a keen eye for the business side of ski resort operations.

Riders blast down the Soaring Eagle ziprider, installed in 2012. It's part of the Cranmore Mountain Adventure Park. Cranmore was named No. 3 in the East for off-hill activities by *Ski Magazine* in 2012. *Photo by Bill Lee, Cranmore Mountain Resort.*

Cranmore's Giant Swing offers year-round thrills for families—part of the resort's Mountain Adventure Park, where riders are encouraged to "find their inner Super Hero." *Photo by Bill Lee, Cranmore Mountain Resort.*

"It took us fourteen months to close this deal, and Steve Rice was an integral part of it with all three of us. There was a great deal of united trust, even though the plan evolved as we went through it," said Brian Fairbank. Added son Tyler, "At the closing, we joked that we ended up with 'version 28.' But in the two years since that, the only deviation has been the decision to add a new triple chair—that wasn't in the original plan [but it was an opportunity that presented itself with the availability of a triple from Wachusett Mountain]."

All the rest—enhanced snow making, the addition of a mountain coaster and the array of other year-round activities—was part of the plan and followed the Jiminy Peak model. "Everything we had done at Jiminy was quickly adaptable here," said Brian Fairbank.

Having a well-respected and liked leader in Wilcox and his team in place, let alone the community connection, made it all the better, noted Brian Fairbank. "Ben's great. To have a proficient leader is not something you can create quickly. To take someone from afar would be really risky," said Brian. He added that he knew and respected Herbert Schneider, having once bunked with him at a PSIA event. His father and uncles all respected

A family enjoys the Giant Swing at Cranmore's Mountain Adventure Park. *Photo by Bill Lee, Cranmore Mountain Resort.*

the Schneiders' role as well. As for the town and mountain relationship, Fairbank said the connection is a gift. "After the sale, they gave me a copy of a painting of the park and the village with the mountain in the background," he said, "and I said, 'Holy Cow!' If you look at that and say there's the community connected to the mountain, and vice versa—well, that's it! I said, wow, this all fits together. When you see the amount of tourism that goes through this valley, you see how this could work. We share that vision, and so does Steve Rice."

"This is our long view," said Tyler, forty-four. "You gotta like us," he laughingly added, "because we're going to be here for the long haul."

Year-Round Fun

The resort has been transformed into a vibrant year-round operation under the new owners, with improvements to the Cranmore Fitness Center, expansion of snow making, retrofitting of the resort's lifts (including the addition of a new $1 million triple to replace the old East Double Chair for 2012–13), expansion of the tubing park to ten lanes and the redesign for 2012–13 of the resort's five terrain parks to more family-friendly cartoon themes.

Other lift changes that have been undertaken by the new owners since 2010 have included the replacement of the old South Double with the installation of a fixed-grip quad that doubled the capacity of the old lift. The South Double was relocated to the Arlberg Children's Center. The center is also serviced by two surface lifts and its own separate beginner's slope.

The upgraded Cranmore Snowsports School features an array of programs for children. The KidsRule Mountain Camps offer one-day instruction. For those who love to run the gates, the Cranmore Race Team offers race programs for older skiers based out of the Cranmore Race

Cranmore's ten-lane snow-tubing park is part of the resort's Mountain Adventure Park. *Photo by Bill Lee, Cranmore Mountain Resort.*

A snowboarder flies through the air at Cranmore Mountain Resort. *Photo by Bill Lee, Cranmore Mountain Resort.*

Center in the old North Chair building. As part of the improvements, a new ticket house was built at the base. The Eating House was also upgraded as Zip's Pub and Grill.

The resort offers Cranapaloozas every Saturday evening throughout the winter, as well as on special nights during vacation weeks. Fireworks are often featured as part of the festivities. Each Cranapalooza is highlighted by face painting, s'mores at the fire pit in Schneider Square, entertainment and more.

Cranmore's Mountain Adventure Center features such family activities as a Mountain Coaster, Giant Swing and the Soaring Eagle zipline, all offered year-round. Winter and summer tubing is also a major draw. Other summer attractions include an aerial ropes course, guided mountain Segway tours, scenic chairlift rides, a Bungy trampoline and a Bouncy House. The Family Fitness Center offers an "Indoor Fun Zone" in winter for families off the slopes, with an adventure course, inflatable Bouncy House, Bungy swing and more. Pizza and other refreshments are available. The center also has two indoor tennis courts, as well as year-round fitness programs and equipment.

The focus on families has earned the resort accolades from several publications in recent years, including *Ski Magazine's Resort Guide for 2012–13*. Cranmore was cited in four categories for Best in the East: second for family programs, third for off-hill activities, seventh for après ski and tenth for terrain parks.

Cranmore is also known for its community partnerships. Every September since 1998, it has served as the venue for Jen's Friends Climb Against Cancer. And every summer it hosts Arts Jubilee, a series of outdoor family concerts.

It's an exciting time for the community and Cranmore as it embarks on its seventy-fifth season.

CHAPTER 14

CHRONOLOGY OF LOCAL SKI HISTORY

- **March 9, 1913**: First recorded use of skis in Tuckerman Ravine by Carl Shumway and five fellow Dartmouth Outing Club (DOC) members. **March 10**: Fred Harris, founder of DOC, and fellow DOC members Shumway and Joseph Cheney make first full ascent and descent of Mount Washington Auto Road on skis.
- **February 1922**: North Conway hosts its first White Mountain Sports Carnival, which includes skijoring on Main Street and ski jumping at the base of Cathedral Ledge.
- **April 11, 1931**: Olympians and Dartmouth Outing Club skiers John Carleton and Charles N. Proctor make the first descent on skis of the Tuckerman Ravine headwall. A week later, on **April 19, 1931**, a group of Harvard skiers—Robert Livermore, Brad Trafford and Robert Balch—becomes the first to ski from the summit down over the headwall.
- **1932**: First Boston and Maine Snow Train visits North Conway (after first New England snow train travels to Warner, New Hampshire, in 1931).
- **1933**: Civilian Conservation Corps cuts ski trails in the White Mountains, including Wildcat Valley Trail in Pinkham Notch.
- **1933, 1934 and 1939**: American Inferno Races held on Mount Washington. Winners are Hollis Phillips ('33), Dick Durrance ('34) and Toni Matt ('39).

- **December 1935**: Edwin Moody, Phil Robertson and George Morton open one of the nation's first overhead cable lifts in Jackson. Bill and Betty Whitney buy Moody's Inn in the fall of 1936; Whitney retrofits the lift with shovel handles in 1937. The lift becomes known as the Shovel Handle.
- **December 1935**: Eastern Slope Ski Club founded.
- **January 1936**: First trail cleared and cabin built by local young volunteers at base of non–lift serviced Mount Cranmore.
- **December 1936**: After breaking his back in a bad fall in April 1934 on the 1933-built Wildcat Ski Trail, Carroll P. Reed, while recuperating, reads about Hannes Schneider's ski school in St. Anton am Arlberg, Austria. With support of the region, Reed founds the American branch of Schneider's ski school in Jackson in December 1936, with Schneider school instructor Benno Rybizka serving as its first director. Carroll and Kay (Damon) Reed found first Carroll Reed's Ski Shop in 1937. Out west, Sun Valley opens with world's first chairlift in 1936, followed by Belknap (now Gunstock) single chair in 1937.
- **January 1937**: Harvey D. Gibson and stepdaughter Whitney Bourne visit Reed's school at Whitneys' (now Black Mountain) in Jackson. Gibson quietly acquires Mount Cranmore.
- **Summer 1937**: Gibson acquires Hotel Randall in North Conway and renames it the Eastern Slope Inn.
- **1937–38**: Cranmore opens, serviced by a rope tow owned by Reed that Gibson paid to have moved from Jackson to Cranmore. Reed establishes a second branch of Eastern Slope Ski School at Cranmore, directed by Rybizka, while fellow Schneider disciple Franz Koessler of St. Anton directs the Jackson branch. Nearby, Pleasant Mountain opens in Bridgton, Maine.
- **January 1938**: Eastern Slope Ski Club Junior Program founded by Chuck Emerson and others.
- **March 1938**: Austrian Anschluss; Hannes Schneider arrested for anti-Nazi views.
- **Summer 1938**: Gibson purchases Reed's ski schools. Work begins on George Morton's Skimobile lift.
- **Summer 1938**: State of New Hampshire opens Cannon Mountain Tramway.
- **December 27, 1938**: Lower Skimobile completed.
- **February 1939**: Famed Austrian skimeister Hannes Schneider released from Nazi custody through Gibson's efforts; Schneider and his family

arrive in North Conway to direct ski schools on February 11. Schneider advises Gibson to expand trails to summit.

- **AUGUST 1939**: Upper Skimobile completed to summit, trails cleared. Gibson Cabin and summit cabin built.
- **1940s**: Cranmore, with its west-facing slopes, heavy skier traffic and solid financial resources, becomes the first ski resort to develop a serious program of snow grooming under the leadership of then mountain manager Phil Robertson (1901–1992).
- **1940–66**: Gibson Trophy Cup Races held. Revived as Master's race in 1989.
- **1945–46**: Lower Skimobile track completely rebuilt; steel runner track installed. New base lodge built.
- **1948**: Black Mountain added next to Whitneys'.
- **SEPTEMBER 11, 1950**: Harvey Dow Gibson, sixty-eight, dies. Helen Gibson directs Skimobile with help of Robertson.
- **APRIL 26, 1955**: Hannes Schneider, sixty-four, dies. Son Herbert Schneider becomes director and president of ski school.
- **DECEMBER 1955**: East Chair and East Slope open; double rope tow replaced by Poma lift on South Slope. About this time, *Today Show* visits Cranmore to film racers, skiers and families riding local inventor Howard Dearborn's Sno-Cat-pulled "Sleighmobile." (To view Dearborn's vintage film footage, visit vimeo.com/47042582 or Google "Howard Dearborn Today Show.")
- **JANUARY 1958**: Wildcat Ski Area opens in Pinkham Notch.
- **DECEMBER 27, 1961**: Skimobile inventor George Morton, seventy, dies.
- **1962**: King Pine Ski Area opens at Purity Spring Resort.
- **1963**: Mrs. Gibson sells Cranmore to Herbert Schneider and four Babco partners of Lynn, Massachusetts.
- **DECEMBER 1963**: North Chair opens on twenty-fifth anniversary of Skimobile.
- **1965**: Phil Robertson opens Attitash in Bartlett, with Thad Thorne as general manager. Les Otten buys it in 1994 and develops Bear Peak with Phil Gravink's direction.
- **1970**: Snow making installed at Cranmore with community support.
- **1971**: Mid-Chair opens.
- **1972**: Local Yokel Recreational Ski League founded by Herbert Schneider and Steve Sherlock. Its name is changed to Mountain Meisters after Sherlock leaves. It is believed to be the largest citizens' weekly recreational ski race program in the nation.

- **1972**: Bretton Woods Ski Area opens, as does Jackson Ski Touring Foundation (JSTF) in Jackson. The JSTF was later joined by such other local touring centers as Bear Notch Ski Touring and Snowshoe Center, Bretton Woods Nordic, Great Glen Trails Outdoor Center, King Pine Nordic Reserve and Mount Washington Valley Ski Touring and Snowshoe Center.
- **1975–84**: Cranmore Tennis Stadium hosts Volvo International Tennis Tournament, won three times by Jimmy Connors.
- **October 1984**: Cranmore purchased by group headed by Ed Mank of Boston. Major capital improvement plan launched.
- **1986–87**: Lookout Triple Chair and new North Base Lodge open. Main Base Lodge is expanded and remodeled. Snow making extended to 100 percent of the mountain. Trailside condominiums built.
- **1987–88**: South Slope Double Chair opens.
- **1988–89**: Cranmore rededicates Skimobile in December and hosts season-long fiftieth-anniversary "Flight Without Wings" celebration of the Schneider family's arrival, culminating in February. Hannes Schneider statue created by sculptor Ed Materson of Cape Elizabeth, Maine, unveiled.
- **1991**: Ed Mank signs three-year management agreement with Bay Bank of Boston.
- **1994**: Sno-Engineering Inc. of Littleton is hired by Bay Bank, with Ken Lydecker hired as interim general manager 1994–95 as the bank seeks a buyer.
- **1995**: Les Otten of LBO Enterprises—owner of Sunday River and Attitash (and pending buyer of Sugarbush)—buys Cranmore in June and installs Skimobile Express high-speed detachable base-to-summit chair. Tim Harris named general manager.
- **November 1996**: Due to a divestiture order from the Department of Justice, Otten's American Skiing Company sells Cranmore and Waterville Valley to George Gillette's Booth Creek Holdings, which operates several areas in the West and Northwest, including Sierra-at-Lake-Tahoe. Snow making is greatly enhanced over the next fourteen years. Booth Creek's Ted Austin named general manager.
- **1996**: Black Mountain acquired by John and Andy Fichera.
- **March 1997**: First Schneider Cup race held at Cranmore as annual fundraiser for New England Ski Museum.
- **2001**: Cranmore opens terrain parks.
- **2004**: Formerly of Attitash and Bretton Woods, Ben Wilcox of North Conway named general manager of Cranmore, succeeding Austin.

- **2007**: Peak Resorts buys Attitash; acquires Wildcat in 2010.
- **DECEMBER 2009**: 2002 Olympic Salt Lake groomer Jimmy Mersereau, longtime Cranmore mountain operations director, dies at age sixty-six. Posthumously awarded Environmental Merit Lifetime Achievement Award by the federal Environmental Protection Agency in 2010 for his pioneering work with biodiesel fuel to power Cranmore's grooming fleet. Jimmy's Run dedicated in his memory in December 2010.
- **JUNE 2010**: Booth Creek sells Cranmore to Brian and Tyler Fairbank and Joe O'Donnell, owners of Jiminy Peak, with capital supplied by CNL Lifestyle Properties Inc., a Florida-based real estate investment trust. Group invests $8.3 million into base and lift improvements. Ownership expands year-round attractions by adding Mountain Adventure Park.
- **JUNE 10, 2012**: Skimeister Herbert Schneider dies at age ninety-two.
- **2012–13**: Seventy-fifth-anniversary season includes January 12, 2013 gala at the Red Jacket; installation of new Schneider Triple, named after Herbert Schneider, to replace East Chair that was retired in March 2012; and redesign of terrain parks, newly focused on families and beginners.

—Compiled 2012 by Tom Eastman

SOURCES AND GENERAL BIBLIOGRAPHY

I have based the majority of my historical research on the same sources that I used to write a book for Mount Cranmore Inc. in 1989, entitled *Flight Without Wings: A Celebration of Hannes Schneider and 50 Years of Skiing at Mt. Cranmore* (Mt. Cranmore Inc., 1989). I have also written extensively on these subjects in articles published by the *Mountain Ear* and the *Conway Daily Sun* since 1979. Where necessary, I have updated those stories for this 2012 publication through additional interviews or by accessing new sources.

A key resource throughout has been Jeff Leich, executive director of the New England Ski Museum (NESM). NESM historian E. John B. Allen has also been of invaluable help. I owe a great debt to the late Herbert Schneider.

Below is a general listing by the book's major topics since the publishing of the 1989 book.

Chapter 1

Gibson, Harvey Dow. *Harvey Dow Gibson, 1882–1950*. "Skiing." N.p., 1951.

Hastings, Peter G. Hastings Law Office PA, Fryeburg, Maine. Interviewed September 2012 about Carroll County Superior Court, Ossipee, NH Equity No. 2298, *Redstone Properties, Inc. v. Cranmore Skimobiles, Inc. Harvey D. Gibson and Helen W. Gibson*. September 29, 1951.

Henney History Room. Cranmore maps, Robert Cottrell and volunteer Lorena Hoyt, interviewed September 2012.

Hounsell, Janet McAllister, and Ruth Burnham Davis Horne. *Conway, New Hampshire: 1765–1997*. Portsmouth, NH: Peter Randall Publisher, 1998.
Reporter. "Boys Build Ski Shelter on Cranmore Trail." January 28, 1937, 3.
———. "Harvey D. Gibson Buys Cranmore Mountain for Public Use."
Westervelt, Carol, Audrey Vorperian and Stefi Reed Hastings. "History of the Eastern Slope Ski Club, 1936–2006." Booklet, ESSC, 2006.

CHAPTER 2

Allen, E. John B., and Jeff Leich, New England Ski Museum.
Smith, Dwight, retired Conway Scenic Railroad president. Interviews with Tom Eastman, 1988 and 2009.

CHAPTER 3

Cummings, Karen. "1936–1986: Jackson Skiing Legends." Official program booklet.
Hastings, Stefi Reed. Interviews with Tom Eastman, summer 2012.
Leich, Jeff. Interview with Tom Eastman, October 2012.
Reed, Carroll P. Numerous interviews with Tom Eastman in the 1980s and early 1990s for the *Mountain Ear* and *Flight Without Wings: A Celebration of Hannes Schneider and 50 Years of Skiing at Mt. Cranmore* (N.p.: Mt. Cranmore Inc., 1989).
———. "Outline for the Winter Season 1936–1937 of the Eastern Slope Ski School." Letter to innkeepers, 1936–37.
Reporter. "Cranmore Slope Enlarged." January 27, 1938, 1.

CHAPTER 4

Eastman, Tom. *Flight Without Wings: A Celebration of Hannes Schneider and 50 Years of Skiing at Mt. Cranmore*. N.p.: Mt. Cranmore Inc., 1989.
Gibson, Harvey Dow. *Harvey Dow Gibson, 1882–1950*. "Skiing." N.p., 1951.

CHAPTER 5

Eastman, Tom. "North Conway's Eastern Slope Inn." *Skiing Heritage* (December 2007).
Gibson, Harvey Dow. *Harvey Dow Gibson, 1882–1950*. "Skiing." N.p., 1951.
Hounsell, Janet McAllister, and Ruth Burnham Davis Horne. *Conway, New Hampshire: 1765–1997*. Portsmouth, NH: Peter Randall Publisher, 1998.
Pinkham, Peter Pinkham. Interview with Tom Eastman, fall 2007.
Reporter. July 1, 1926, and July 1937.

Chapter 6

Holmes, John "Hot Rod." Interview with Tom Eastman, September 2012.

Miller, Marilyn, former general manager. Interview with Tom Eastman at Cranmore, July 2012.

Chapter 7

Allen, E. John B. "Hannes Schneider and the Germans." *Journal of the New England Ski Museum* 65 (Summer 2006): 24–26.

Fairlie, Gerard, and Bill Clapp. *Flight Without Wings*. N.p., 1957.

Chapter 8

Schneider, Herbert. Interviews with Tom Eastman and Jeff Leich at Schneider residence, St. Anton am Arlberg, Austria, April 2005. (Herbert Schneider was interviewed extensively by Eastman over the years 1985 to 2012.)

Chapter 9

Dolan, Karen. Interview with Tom Eastman at Cranmore, August 2012.

Smith, Leanne. Responded to request to submit an e-mail correspondence to author Tom Eastman, September 2012, on Eastern Slope Ski Club Junior Program and Herbert Schneider.

Chapter 10

Leich, Jeff. *Over the Headwall: The Ski History of Tuckerman Ravine*. N.p.: New England Ski Museum, 1999. Second edition 2011. 76–88.

Matt, Toni. Interviews with Tom Eastman over the phone in summer 1988 and in person in February 1989. Stories published in the *Mountain Ear* in 1989 and the *Conway Daily Sun's Valley Fun* in 2009.

Schneider, Herbert. Interviews with Tom Eastman at Cranmore, March 2009.

Chapter 11

Bennett, Kathy. Interview with Tom Eastman at Cranmore about late Jimmy Mersereau, September 2012.

Phillips, Drew. Interview with Tom Eastman by phone, October 2012.

Styffe, Eric. Interview with Tom Eastman by phone, October 2012.

Wilcox, Ben. Interview with Tom Eastman, August 2012.

Chapter 12

Gravink, Phil. Interview with Tom Eastman by phone from his Jackson home, August 2012.

Mank, Ed. Interview with Tom Eastman by phone, October 2012.

Miller, Marilyn. Interview with Tom Eastman by phone, October 2012.

Mountain Ear, *Conway Daily Sun* and *Lewiston Sun Journal* files on Department of Justice divestiture filings and sales of Cranmore over the years since the publication in 1989 of *Flight Without Wings: A Celebration of Hannes Schneider and 50 Years of Skiing at Mt. Cranmore.*

Rice, Steve. Interview with Tom Eastman by phone, September 2012.

Wilcox, Ben, Tyler Fairbank and Brian Fairbank. Interview with Tom Eastman at Cranmore, September 2012.

Chapter 13

Bennett, Kathy. Cranmore 2012–13 Media Kit.

Fairbank, Brian, Tyler Fairbank and Ben Wilcox. Interview with Tom Eastman, October 2012.

Chapter 14

Eastman, Tom. *Flight Without Wings: A Celebration of Hannes Schneider and 50 Years of Skiing at Mt. Cranmore* (1989), with updates from *Mountain Ear* and *Conway Daily Sun* files.

ABOUT THE AUTHOR

Tom Eastman, fifty-five, is a longtime journalist in Mount Washington Valley. He and his late brother, Steve Eastman (1949–2008), worked together at the *Mountain Ear* from 1979 to 2007. He joined the staff at the *Conway Daily Sun* in 2007 and serves as a reporter as well as co-editor of the paper's *Valley Fun* tourist publication. He also has done radio work as "The Valley Voice" for local radio station WMWV 93.5-FM. He has written for several magazines and publications, including *Yankee*, the *Montreal Gazette*, *Powder* and *Skiing Heritage*. He studied journalism at the University of New Hampshire under late renowned writing instructor Donald Murray, graduating in 1979.

Writer Tom Eastman (right) is shown with author and ski historian Jeff Leich (left) of the New England Ski Museum and the late Herbert Schneider near the Sporthaus Schneider in St. Anton am Arlberg, Austria, in 2005. *Photo by Christoph Schneider.*

Eastman was named a White Mountain Treasure in October 2010 by the Mount Washington Valley Chamber of Commerce for his excellence in journalism and community activism.

A member of the Eastern Ski Writers Association, Eastman won an Excellence in Newspaper Features Writing Award for 2009–10 from the North American Snowsports Journalists Association. He is also a two-time runner-up for that award. He was named Ski NH's Media Person of the Year in 2001. He received Berwick Academy's Distinguished Alumni Award for his writing in 2002. He has lectured on ski history both in the United States and Austria, including at the 2002 International Ski History Congress in Park City, Utah, and at a 2005 international forum in St. Anton am Arlberg, Austria, on the fiftieth anniversary of Hannes Schneider's death. He authored a book, *Flight Without Wings: A Celebration of Hannes Schneider and 50 Years of Skiing at Mt. Cranmore*, in 1989. He contributed a chapter on Conway history to the fifty-essay book *Beyond the Notches: Stories of Place in New Hampshire's North Country*, which won an "Outstanding Work of Non-Fiction" award from the New Hampshire Writers' Project in 2011.

Eastman is an avid alpine and cross-country skier who takes to the tracks and trails as often as he can.